CW00544782

Shahar Marcus
Valeria Monis

TEL AVIV

FOOD. PEOPLE. STORIES.

A culinary journey with

NENI

With recipes from Haya Molcho & Elihay Biran,
stories by Ellen Lewis & Walther Hetzer
and photographs by Nuriel Molcho

MURDOCH BOOKS
SYDNEY · LONDON

bon-bon
$ATM€
YAMISAGI

CONTENTS

TEL AVIV
FOOD. PEOPLE. STORIES.

HAYA

Name: Haya Molcho
My Role at NENI: The soul of the business
My Favourite Place in Tel Aviv:
Shuk Ha'Carmel – the Carmel Market
My Favourite Food: Eggplant from a wood-fired oven
My Tel Aviv Story: The most frequently used word during the production of the book was ›Yalla‹ – short for: we have to hurry!

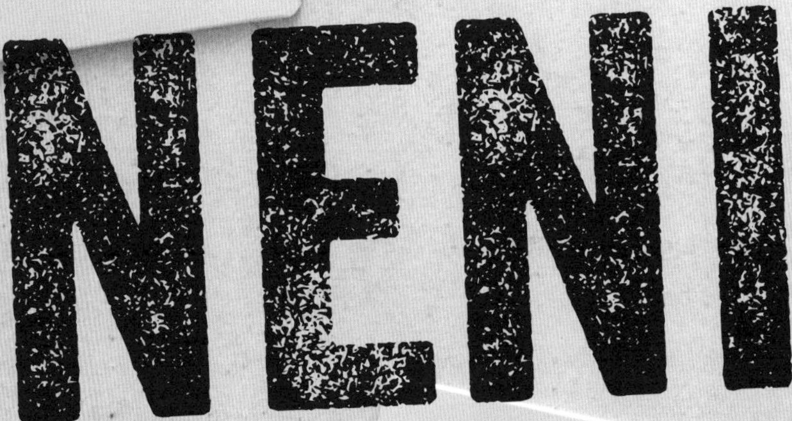

Name: Elior Molcho
My Role at NENI: General Manager, Project Manager and responsible for human resources management
My Favourite Place in Tel Aviv:
Teder (page 102)
My Favourite Food: Sabich
My Tel Aviv Story: I had a great time with my family in Israel – where the roots of our cooking tradition are. I am pleased that through this book even more people will get to see some of the wonderful sides of Tel Aviv.

ELIOR

NURIEL

Name: Nuriel Molcho
My Role at NENI: PR & Marketing and the photographer for this book
My Favourite Place in Tel Aviv: The market in Jaffa for breakfast and the promenade for sunset walks
My Favourite Food: Sabich, a classic street food. Every bite contains the full flavour of Israel – I always order it with plenty of amba and zhug.
My Tel Aviv Story: What I enjoyed most was spending so much time in Tel Aviv. Often when I go there I arrive and have to quickly depart again. This time I could settle in and really feel at home.

Name: Ilan Molcho
My Role at NENI: CEO & CFO
My Favourite Place in Tel Aviv: Port Said (page 102)
My Favourite Food: Octopus salad with celery, oranges and potatoes
My Tel Aviv Story: What I loved most was the spontaneity. On one of our last days in Tel Aviv, we organised a small party in the kitchen, and each of us invited a few friends. Those friends brought other friends with them, and suddenly there were 200 people in front of the kitchen, partying with us until three in the morning. That is how it should be. Chaotic, sympathetic, good people, good food, a lot of dancing. Simply BALAGAN!

ILAN

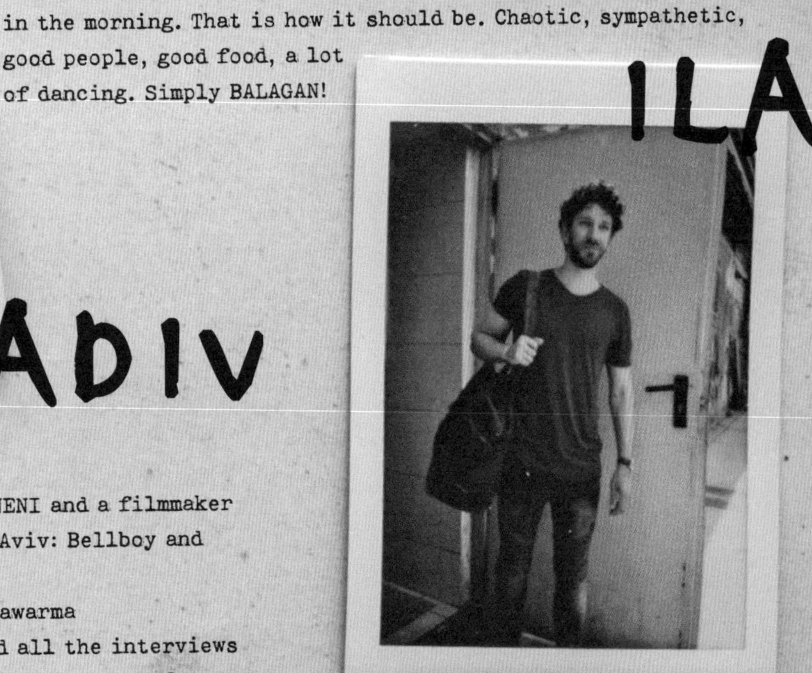

NADIV

Name: Nadiv Molcho
My Role at NENI: An 'N' in NENI and a filmmaker
My Favourite Place in Tel Aviv: Bellboy and Frishman Beach
My Favourite Food: Pita shawarma
My Tel Aviv Story: I filmed all the interviews and behind the scenes as well – the result was the book trailer.

קונה תקליטים
052-7025320 רז
3=100
BEATLES

TEL AVIV
FOOD. PEOPLE. STORIES.

The atmosphere of any city is the result of the memories and dreams of the people who live there, of their hopes, worries, successes and opportunities. It also comes from its sights, sounds and smells – and this is especially true of Tel Aviv. The city's very name contains poetry: *Tel* makes one think of old hills, of millennia-old remains, while *Aviv* signifies spring and new beginnings. This is a city full of contrasts. Its diversity of experiences and people creates a complex mosaic in which new impulses act on cultures and traditions from around the world.

For this book, we set off together on a discovery tour through Tel Aviv. We love the synergy between regional culinary roots and the new, innovative ideas that we feel very distinctly here. The markets of Tel Aviv are noisy hubs of activity, with Yemeni, Turkish and Iraqi businesses often standing side by side, while in the city's restaurants, the mixture of culinary influences from the entire world arrives right at your table. Street food is ubiquitous and brings people together through the intimacy of having food placed in one's hands. It is in this vibrant community that we found our interview partners, who graciously and openly talked about their lives with us.

For two weeks, in preparing for this book, we lived in the rhythm of this city. All of the dishes were prepared here, all the ingredients were purchased fresh at the markets, and we met our interview partners at the places where they live and work. We were able to visit an eighth-generation Arab fisherman on his trawler and his younger Jewish collaborator who supplies fish to the city's top restaurants. We rode around Tel Aviv with a blogging taxi driver. We received a warm welcome both at a traditional bakery run by Uzbek immigrants and at a stylish patisserie that wouldn't be out of place in Paris. Through all of the people we met and places we visited, we found something of the distinctive character of this wonderful city and gained historical and sociological insights into its culinary traditions and latest trends.

Tel Aviv is also the city where Haya was born and raised. From her early childhood, she has particularly vivid memories of the colourful stands of the street vendors where the sweet and refreshing cactus fruit known as sabra was piled high on a bed of ice blocks. And of tiras, corn cobs grilled over an open fire on the beach. Samy, Haya's husband and a famous pantomime, also has very clear memories of his early years in Tel Aviv. Eighty years ago, he grew up in the drained swamp on the border to Jaffa and watched as the ›White City‹ grew on the other side. He remembers the smell of the earth on Shabbat, when the streets were sprinkled with water, and the waves of immigrants who have been bringing their own culture and food with them for over sixty years. In the 1930s and '40s, many people came here from Germany and the rest of Europe, later from Yemen, Iraq and other Arab countries, and then from Russia and Ethiopia. Each group brought its artists, singers and actors to Tel Aviv. Today the artistic trends and innovations of this city make themselves felt throughout the world. In this way, Tel Aviv has been and remains an inexhaustible source of inspiration, and we return to this city again and again.

There are so many similarities between NENI and the people of Tel Aviv whom we describe: we are spontaneous risk-takers; we have a penchant for improvisation and are continually incorporating new experiences into our work. NENI is a family enterprise: in 2009, we opened our first restaurant on Vienna's Naschmarkt; the first letters of the names of Haya's four sons – Nuriel, Elior, Nadiv and Ilan – form the restaurant's name. NENI brought a special and distinctive culinary touch to Vienna,

a laid-back mixture of Mediterranean and Levantine food culture. We all contribute our talents to the business and are in constant communication with each other. NENI has now grown into a Europe-wide brand, with restaurants, a cooking school, its own line of products - and cookbooks. Despite this expansion process, we have remained an informal, lively group of people who enjoy this close collaboration and exchange of ideas.

During our time in Tel Aviv, we visited restaurants and the people behind them, which we selected because they demonstrated particular passion and creativity. We present classic restaurants but also introduce a trend that is steadily growing in this city: restaurants and jobs that defy traditional definitions. Some are pop-ups, launched by young people who do not have the money to renovate and maintain a large restaurant or perhaps are not willing to sacrifice their private lives to the harsh laws of the restaurant business. Instead, they open temporary restaurants – whether in their own apartment, as part of a cultural event, or as a joint project with other cooks. Sometimes the projects develop into something more, and the restaurants remain at a location permanently; other times people choose to move on to their next project. But what they all have in common is great dedication, energy, and a passion for what they do. During our stay, we were fortunate to become part of this new scene, creating our own temporary restaurant at Burek (page 27).

After all the food had been cooked and photographed, all the interviews had been conducted and all the locations visited, we wanted to show our appreciation by inviting the people involved in the making of this book to celebrate with us. Burek was bursting at the seams that evening; food was prepared, people met for the first time, new ideas were born, and music and drinks flowed until late in the night. And many came: friends, family members and everyone who so graciously opened their kitchens and their hearts, who took time for us, and who allowed us to portray them in this book.

No one has to be especially encouraged to talk in Tel Aviv, and as soon as people sit down together at a table, not only is food shared but also ideas, stories, opinions and recipes. This is the spirit of life that we have captured for you in this book and that we would like to bring into your home. For this book we cooked, baked and tasted, but we also philosophised and laughed about life. And we believe that the character of Tel Aviv, this constantly evolving city, exists here in our recipes as well as in the stories and memories of its people.

Bon appétit! B'tai Avon!

NENI

The NENI team

אינסטלטור
קוטיק דוד

VEGETABLES, GRAINS & LEGUMES

SABICH, SARMA AND MORE

AVOCADO SANDWICH WITH PICKLED CARROTS

For 4 people for breakfast
or a light meal

For the pickled carrots:
- O 10 carrots (approx. 500 g/1 lb 2 oz)
- O 2 sprigs dill
- O 1 sprig coriander (cilantro)
- O 2 garlic cloves
- O 300 ml (10½ fl oz) white vinegar
- O 1 dried red chilli, or 1 pinch chilli flakes
- O 50 g (1¾ oz) sugar
- O 1 teaspoon sea salt
- O ½ teaspoon black peppercorns
- O 6 cardamom pods
- O ½ teaspoon coriander seeds

For the garlic cream:
- O 1 garlic clove
- O 1 shallot
- O 100 g (3½ oz) crème fraîche
- O 1 tablespoon lemon juice
- O ½ teaspoon sea salt

For the avocados:
- O 2 avocados
- O 1 tablespoon lime juice
- O ½ teaspoon sea salt
- O 1 tablespoon olive oil

- O 2 tablespoons pepitas (pumpkin seeds)
- O 4 slices challa (see page 253)

Peel *carrots*. Slice into thin strips with a vegetable peeler and layer in a large glass jar. Add the dill and coriander.

Peel and finely chop the garlic. Bring the vinegar, chilli, sugar, salt, peppercorns, cardamom, coriander seeds, garlic and 250 ml (9 fl oz) water to the boil in a small pan and simmer until the sugar has dissolved. Pour the hot liquid over the carrots, seal the jar and leave overnight at room temperature.

The next day, peel and finely chop the garlic and shallot for the *garlic cream*. Mix together all ingredients and season to taste.

Halve the *avocados* and remove the stones. Using a spoon, cut out crescent-shaped pieces and mix with the lime juice, salt and olive oil.

Dry-roast the pepitas in a small frying pan until crispy. Toast the challa and spread with the garlic cream. Cut the challa slices in half. Top half of the slices with avocado and carrot strips. Sprinkle with pepitas and place the other halves of the bread on top.

HAYA'S TIP:
CARROTS CAN BE PICKLED AND KEPT IN A SEALED JAR IN THE REFRIGERATOR FOR UP TO A MONTH. THEY GO WITH ANY FOOD THAT YOU WOULD LIKE TO INFUSE WITH A SWEET-SOUR NOTE.

Even today, breakfast for Haya and her husband, Samy, consists of an avocado and good sourdough bread. The avocado is a food that bears the flavour of Haya's childhood in Israel. The pickled carrots and the garlic, on the other hand, are ubiquitous in Romania. Each year, Haya's grandmother preserved cucumbers, capsicums (peppers), cauliflower, beetroot and cabbage. The large canning jars stood on the table at every meal.

This sandwich combines different consistencies (creamy and crispy), flavours (the slight sweetness of the avocado, the acidity of the carrots and the pungency of the garlic) and Haya's Israeli memories with her Romanian roots. It is also on the NENI breakfast menu and an absolute hit with customers.

GRILLED CORN WITH CHILLI BUTTER

For 4 people as an appetiser
for outdoor barbecues

For the chilli butter:
- 125 g (4½ oz) butter
- 1 large fresh red chilli
- 25 g (1 oz) muscovado sugar

- 4 corn cobs, with husk
- Sea salt
- 1 handful basil

In Tel Aviv, corn – called *tiras* in Hebrew – is often cooked on the beach in large pots over an open fire. The husks remain on the cobs while they are cooked and are removed before serving. This is what gives the corn its fabulous flavour. And the aroma is extraordinary! After Haya's family moved to Bremen, it was not only the people they missed in Germany but also many foods from Israel, including corn. For this reason, every time Haya visited Tel Aviv she was greeted at the airport by family members and friends with corn and the equally beloved prickly pears.

Grilled corn is now served at Vienna's Tel Aviv Beach as well – and cooked in the traditional manner over an open fire.

Melt *butter* in a small pan. Deseed the chilli and purée along with the sugar in a blender or with a stick blender to make a paste. Add the melted butter and continue blending until the mixture is smooth and creamy.

Place the corn, in the husk, in a large saucepan and add sufficient water to cover. Season with salt, bring to the boil and cook for about 30 minutes.

Remove corn from the water and drain. Roast on a charcoal grill or over an open fire until dark brown.

Husk the corn and coat with the chilli butter. Slice the basil into thin strips and sprinkle over the corn.

THE INQUISITIVE CHEF

burek_tlv

BARAK YEHEZKELI

Burek

»The Inquisitive Chef«

A dense jumble of low sheds, most of them single-storey workshops for artisans, and narrow alleyways covered with graffiti mark a neighbourhood that has now become an urban hub of creativity: this is Florentin. The sun is shining as we walk past a carpentry shop and arrive at Ha Nagarim Street 14. On a patio overhung with flowers stands a long table next to a somewhat dilapidated piano. The smell of sawdust mingles with the aroma of fresh herbs.

We enter a large industrial space that was once the studio of a famous Israeli artist and now houses a spacious open kitchen with state-of-the-art equipment. At the work areas, spices and fresh vegetables wait to be processed. Beautiful old enamel and porcelain dishes are stacked on flea-market tables, and the shelves on the back wall are lined with award-winning Israeli wines. This is Burek, a unique kitchen and restaurant, which serves as a space for private functions and a forum for chefs to exchange ideas and experiment. One night a week, it is transformed into a first-class restaurant overseen by Head Chef and creator, Barak Yehezkeli. Burek served as NENI's base in Tel Aviv. We also had the privilege of playing host along with Barak for one evening.

This incredible location, just what we had been looking for in Tel Aviv to serve as our home base, is where the recipes for this book were created. For two weeks, we were at Burek virtually night and day – it became our home away from home. From the planning and the daily food shopping at the markets with Barak's team to the final party, everything happened from here. Haya, Elihay and Adrian wrote recipes and cooked, Nuriel arranged and photographed the dishes, and on many evenings we all sat around the patio table, laughing and eagerly tasting the day's ›work‹. The connection we made with Barak during our time together in Tel Aviv became a bond of friendship half a year later when Barak and an Israeli film crew landed in Vienna to spend days with Haya in her own element, filming her for a segment of Barak's new multi-episode cooking show about eight Israeli cooks who have made a name for themselves outside of Israel. Barak, who founded Burek along with his partner Jonathan Bergman, is exceedingly charming and looks quite a bit younger than his nearly 45 years. He is personable and welcoming as we settle in for our chat, and in a city where most people express themselves volubly, he is calm and speaks softly. We find a spot for our interview in the gallery above the kitchen. Below us, fish and asparagus are being grilled and the aroma of caramelised onions wafts up to us. In another corner, a team is making arrangements and compiling shopping lists for the photo shoot the following day.

As with many of the people we have interviewed in Tel Aviv, we begin with Barak's roots. His ancestors came from Bukhara in Uzbekistan, Kurdistan and Spain. In the corner stands the rocking chair in which his mother breastfed him. ›Food is the first link to other people in a baby's life,‹ he says. Foods from his childhood in Haifa are an important part of his identity because everyone in his family cooked. He remembers that every Saturday his Kurdish grandma would serve him a freshly baked, golden-brown challa with pickles for breakfast. Nearly as often there was *sofrito*, a slowly boiled dish made of beef and potatoes – classic ›slow food‹. Immediately, a lively discussion ensues about the name of this dish, which has nothing to do with the Italian *soffrito*, made with quickly sautéed garlic, carrot, onion and other vegetables.

Barak's father was an artist who studied engineering and worked internationally in sales. He took his son on many trips, and Barak tells us that he always

»Cooking requires chutzpah.«

›decoded‹ the world by way of its food traditions. Barak has retained his vivid interest in different cultures. After the army and engineering studies at the prestigious Technion, he was looking for a new focus. He spent a year in India where he remembers places in which only yoghurt and paneer were available; he made his own cheese and gnocchi and discovered the use of zucchini (courgette) flowers for tempura. He travelled on to Thailand to spend a week cleaning a beach but ended up in the kitchen of a beach restaurant instead. Still searching, he somehow found himself, together with his girlfriend, in Boston in the middle of winter – in flip-flops! There he gained his first professional experience in a French restaurant, which opened up still another world of food artistry for him. He spent his free time in libraries studying books about cooking.

From Boston, Barak moved on to Tel Aviv. ›Tel Aviv is not Israel – it is a place for people with a curiosity about everything, for creating a new world, a place of freedom.‹ He finds the Israelis here to be very direct, innovative and determined. They live on the edge, learn quickly and have the courage to make mistakes. Barak soon found work because he was ›good with a knife‹. The girlfriend who accompanied him on his trip to Asia and the U.S. has now been his wife for 20 years.

Tel Aviv is often hectic, but in the kitchen Barak takes a quiet and serene approach. His credo is: ›There is no such thing as Israeli cuisine.‹ Influences come from all over, and there have been many changes and innovations in the past 20 years. At Burek, the chefs are free to break all conventional culinary rules. ›Cooking requires chutzpah,‹ says Barak. ›It is OK for it to be a bit brash and very personal.‹

›Passion, love and patience‹ are the words Barak uses to describe his cooking. It is important to him to have an awareness of everything he does: gestures and movements count, as does the connection with nature and with the ingredients. ›Even a dish you make every day will always change.‹ It is important to know where a potato comes from, when it was harvested and how it was stored. He raves about a small squash from Jericho that is watered only with rainwater, giving it its distinctive taste. Barak knows exactly where to find what he is looking for at the markets and out in nature. He uses vegetables grown locally and has berries picked only when they are properly ripe.

Burek celebrates the bond that is created between people through eating. ›I want to watch the people as they bite into their food,‹ says Barak with a laugh. This is where cooks, friends and guests meet; there are no separated areas. In the evening, local kids play soccer across the street on the urban field, and the narrow graffiti-covered alleys of Florentin are silhouetted against the Tel Aviv high-rises in the background. Barak believes that ›food has soul‹. We found that the community-focused place he has created here has plenty of ›soul‹ as well.

In Palestine freekeh was and is a way of using the green, unripe grains of durum wheat. When they are harvested, they are piled in the field, set on fire in the evening and left to smoulder overnight. Because of the high humidity, the grains don't actually burn but are slowly roasted. The next day the ash is washed off and the grains are used whole like rice or ground into flour. Freekeh has a nutty and slightly smoky taste and is particularly popular in the eastern Mediterranean region, although it

ARTICHOKES WITH FREEKEH

For 4 people as an appetiser or a light main dish

For the freekeh:

- 120 g (4¼ oz) freekeh
- 1 tablespoon olive oil
- 1 teaspoon sea salt

For the artichokes:

- 4 large artichokes
- Juice of 1 lemon
- 100 g (3½ oz) small shallots
- 5 garlic cloves
- 5 tablespoons olive oil
- 1 teaspoon chilli flakes
- 400 ml (14 fl oz) vegetable broth (page 113)
- Small handful parsley
- 60 g (2¼ oz) butter
- Sea salt
- Black pepper

- 25 g (1 oz) pecans
- 50 g (1¾ oz) shaved parmesan

Place *freekeh* in a bowl, cover with cold water and stir well with a spoon. Skim off any foam that rises to the surface. Then strain the freekeh through a sieve.

Heat olive oil in a saucepan, add the freekeh and stir well so the grains are completely coated with oil. Add 180 ml (5¾ fl oz) of water, and salt, and bring to the boil. Simmer, covered, over low heat until the freekeh is soft and the water has been completely absorbed, about 20 minutes.

While the freekeh cooks, trim the *artichokes*. Using a serrated knife, cut off most of the stem and the upper two-thirds of the leaves. Place the artichokes on a board with the cut surface down and cut off any hard exterior parts. Then use a small paring knife to remove all remaining hard, dark-green bits and to shape the artichokes into nicely rounded forms. Now carefully scrape out the furry choke with a small spoon or knife. Immediately place the trimmed artichokes in a bowl of water mixed with the lemon juice (reserving 1 tablespoon) so they do not discolour.

Peel and quarter the shallots. Peel the garlic and cut into thin slices. Heat olive oil in a pan, add the artichokes and shallots and sauté until golden brown, 5–8 minutes. Add the garlic and chilli flakes and sauté another minute. Deglaze with the vegetable broth and boil over high heat to reduce by half.

Pluck the parsley leaves from the stems, coarsely chop and stir into the artichokes along with the butter and the 1 tablespoon reserved lemon juice. Continue to reduce until the sauce is thick and creamy. Season to taste with salt and pepper.

Dry-roast the pecans in a frying pan and chop into coarse pieces.

Remove the artichokes from the sauce and arrange on plates. Shape the freekeh into small balls, using two spoons, and place on the artichokes. Drizzle with the sauce and garnish with the pecans and parmesan.

FREEKEH WITH DATES AND NUTS

For 4–6 people as a main dish

For the freekeh:

- O 500 g (1 lb 2 oz) freekeh
- O 25 ml (¾ fl oz) olive oil, plus extra for drizzling
- O ½ teaspoon cumin seeds
- O 2 tablespoons sea salt
- O 100 g (3½ oz) walnuts
- O 100 g (3½ oz) pecans
- O 150 g (5½ oz) medjool dates
- O 1 celery stalk, with greens
- O 50 g (1¾ oz) flat-leaf parsley
- O 50 g (1¾ oz) coriander (cilantro)
- O 25 g (1 oz) mint
- O 1 acri sivri (cayenne) pepper
- O 1 small red onion
- O 500 g (1 lb 2 oz) Greek yoghurt

For the dressing:

- O 40 g (1½ oz) fresh ginger
- O 3 garlic cloves
- O 30 ml (1 fl oz) date syrup, maple syrup or molasses
- O 25 ml (¾ fl oz) lemon juice, plus extra to taste
- O 1 tablespoon balsamic vinegar
- O 1 heaped teaspoon ground cinnamon
- O ½ teaspoon sea salt
- O 125 ml (4 fl oz) olive oil

Place *freekeh* in a bowl, cover with cold water and stir well with a spoon. Skim off any foam that rises to the surface. Then strain the freekeh through a sieve.

Heat olive oil in a saucepan, add the cumin and sauté. Add the freekeh and sauté briefly as well. Add 750 ml (26 fl oz) of water and the salt. Bring to the boil, cover and simmer over low heat until the freekeh is cooked but still al dente and the water has completely evaporated, around 15–20 minutes. Then leave to cool.

Coarsely chop walnuts and pecans; pit and finely dice the dates. Finely dice the celery and chop the celery greens. Pluck the herb leaves from the stems and finely chop. Deseed the sivri pepper and slice into thin strips. Peel the onion and finely dice. In a large bowl, mix together all ingredients for the salad except the yoghurt.

For the *dressing,* peel the ginger and garlic and chop very finely or grate. Whisk together all ingredients except the oil. Pour in the oil slowly in a thin stream and whisk the dressing until it is thick. Pour over the salad and toss well. Season to taste with salt and lemon juice.

To serve, spread the yoghurt on the plates, arrange the freekeh salad on top and drizzle with olive oil.

ROASTED EGGPLANT WITH ASIAN TAHINI

For 4 people as an appetiser

- O 4 eggplant (aubergines)
- O 1 spring onion (scallion), green parts
- O 1 shallot
- O 1 acri sivri (cayenne) pepper
- O 1 pinch sea salt
- O 1 tablespoon olive oil
- O 8 cherry tomatoes
- O 3 sprigs coriander (cilantro)

For the Asian tahini:

- O 1 garlic clove
- O 15 g (½ oz) fresh ginger
- O 1 bird's eye chilli
- O 70 g (2½ oz) pure tahini (sesame seed paste)
- O 70 ml (2¼ fl oz) soy sauce
- O 35 ml (1 fl oz) mirin
- O 1 tablespoon rice vinegar
- O 20 g (¾ oz) sugar
- O 50 ml (1½ fl oz) lime juice
- O 360 ml (12 fl oz) canola or grape seed oil

HAYA'S TIPS:
I USUALLY ROAST THE EGGPLANT OVER THE GAS FLAME, WHICH GIVES IT A SMOKY TASTE. IT IS BEST, OF COURSE, TO DO THIS OUTSIDE ON A CHARCOAL GRILL.

THE TAHINI ALSO GOES WELL WITH A SUMMERY TOMATO SALAD, WHICH THEN TAKE ON A WHOLE NEW AND EXCITING FLAVOUR.

Roast the eggplant whole. For this, place a metal splatter screen over the flame of a gas stove and char the eggplant on it, turning several times, for 10–15 minutes. You can also do this in the oven, placing the eggplant on the top rack and using the grill to roast it on all sides. The skin of the eggplant should be burnt but the inside soft. Peel while still hot.

While the eggplant cooks, trim the green parts of the spring onion and slice into paper-thin strips. Peel the shallot and dice very finely. Deseed the sivri pepper, dice very finely and mix with the salt and olive oil. Cut off the top part of the tomatoes, squeeze out the seeds and reserve. Pluck the coriander leaves from the stems.

For the *Asian tahini,* peel the garlic and ginger and chop very finely. Deseed the chilli and chop very finely as well. In a tall container, mix all the ingredients together except the oil. Pour in oil slowly and whirl with a stick blender until smooth and homogeneous.

Halve the eggplant and arrange on plates. Drizzle with the tahini mixture and garnish with the diced shallot, marinated sivri pepper, tomato seeds, spring onion greens and coriander.

R

THE NAVIGATOR

Gett
THULE

KOBI RUBIN

Taxi Driver and Food Blogger
»The Navigator«

Where do you find good food in Tel Aviv that is served with pride and is also affordable? Our taxi driver, Kobi Rubin, knows because he has a side job: for his highly popular food blog he explores and pays homage to eating places off the beaten track, with high quality and low prices determining the route. Kobi loves eating, talking and writing in equal measure. A self-taught writer, he converses with ease in superb English, a language that he ›somehow learned from TV‹ after he left school at age sixteen. Driving taxis can be a lonely job, so Kobi's culinary excursions also provide him with social interaction.

›Tel Aviv is one big village,‹ Kobi says. He navigates this city both in his taxi and through his weekly food blog with enthusiasm, inside knowledge and a great sense of humour. He criticises the high prices at upscale restaurants, although he admits with a wink that he occasionally eats there himself. When Kobi tests a restaurant he initially remains anonymous and only introduces himself after his blog article goes online. He is not interested in getting a free meal as thanks for positive reviews, or in personal fame; he wants to help those who cannot afford PR and to pay appropriate tribute to good, affordable food. In each place he shows us today, he is greeted very warmly, and so are we as visitors. Today we will spend an entire morning driving with him through the city. The heavy traffic between stops gives us the chance to hear about Kobi's life and family. We will hear a great deal today because Kobi only stops talking long enough to catch a breath.

Memories of his grandfather bring a smile to Kobi's face: his grandfather emigrated from Germany to Tunis, where he had two wives. Kobi's parents came to Israel in the 1950s, and he describes himself as ›three-quarters Tunisian, with a little Ashkenazi‹. Kobi was born in Tel Aviv and now has four children. Another big smile: ›From only one wife!‹ Kobi's wife is a teacher and his oldest son is now eighteen and in the army. ›Then he will study – I don't want him to become a taxi driver.‹

Our first stop is a small stand in the Shuk Ha'Carmel. Kobi worries that this central and lively market might be turning ›posh‹. It may be, but there is no danger of that at Roni Basarim's modest stand:

the beef and chicken kebabs as well as the spicy merguez sausages come directly from the charcoal grill and are served as sandwiches or on a plate with pickled cucumbers and other vegetables. With the stand located right at the entrance to a side alley where butcher shops are lined up cheek by jowl (a single fish merchant has somehow ended up here as well), there can be no question about the quality and freshness of Roni's meats.

This is a busy corner. There are three seats at the small counter and a few stand-up tables on the other side of the narrow alley, where we manage to get a spot. Next to us flows a steady stream of people doing their shopping. Kobi keeps bringing fully laden plates over to us and jokes with all the people standing around. When a supplier turns into the alley with his small delivery truck, everything comes to a standstill. Another customer's scooter falls over, his groceries roll across the ground, and the noise reaches new heights. Surrounded by this cheery chaos, we thoroughly enjoy Roni's inexpensive and delicious food.

Our next stop takes us to the southern part of the city, to Shazar Street in Abu Khabir, where many Jews from Uzbekistan have settled. Kobi promises us a ›bakery with a twist‹. It would be easy to miss the Bukhara bakery, but it attracts a constant flow of customers. Kobi receives a warm welcome.

Irina is in charge here. Her parents founded the bakery after leaving Uzbekistan in 1984 and settling in Tel Aviv. Her father still comes to the shop every evening. Irina is a warm-hearted, strong-willed and lively hostess. She directs us to one of the small outside tables and sees to it that we get something to eat right away: for her, food comes first, then conversation. She brings out plates with hot pasties, some filled with beef; others with black pepper, mashed potatoes and pumpkin; still others with spinach and nuts. This is served with hot green tea and rock sugar on a small plate. Irina insists that we do not put this sugar in our tea but let it melt on our tongue, ›like in Bukhara‹.

The glass storefront displays neatly stacked pyramids of freshly baked breads and other specialties; customers place their orders through the open window. Nothing here in front hints at the wonders that lie behind the small shop. Irina's eyes light up with pride as she leads us to the back area. From an Abu Khabir parking lot, we enter a timeless Central Asian bakery where Uzbek bakers, heads wrapped in cloth turbans, shape dough into large circular flat loaves. A few older women are seated there as well, perhaps just for the company. Two dome-shaped brick ovens occupy pride of place. They are fired from below and the doors are open to the front. Fascinated, we observe the spectacle that follows: the bakers pitch the bread loaves with a good deal of velocity against the interior walls of the oven, where the dough immediately sticks. The doors are closed, and the temperature inside now reaches about 400°C (750°F). Two bakers on their knees monitor the oven, using mirrors through the open bottom, always ready to adjust the heat if needed. There is absolutely no way Irina would let us leave now – we must stay to try the fresh bread! After about ten minutes, the fragrant, hot loaves are peeled off the oven walls and lined up on long shelves. We are given a taste as soon as it can be touched, and it is heavenly. It's time for us to move on, and Irina regrets that her father did not meet us. But she sends us on our way with two fresh loaves of bread.

On the way to the next stop, we drive through streets with small, older houses that were used by

03-5183924

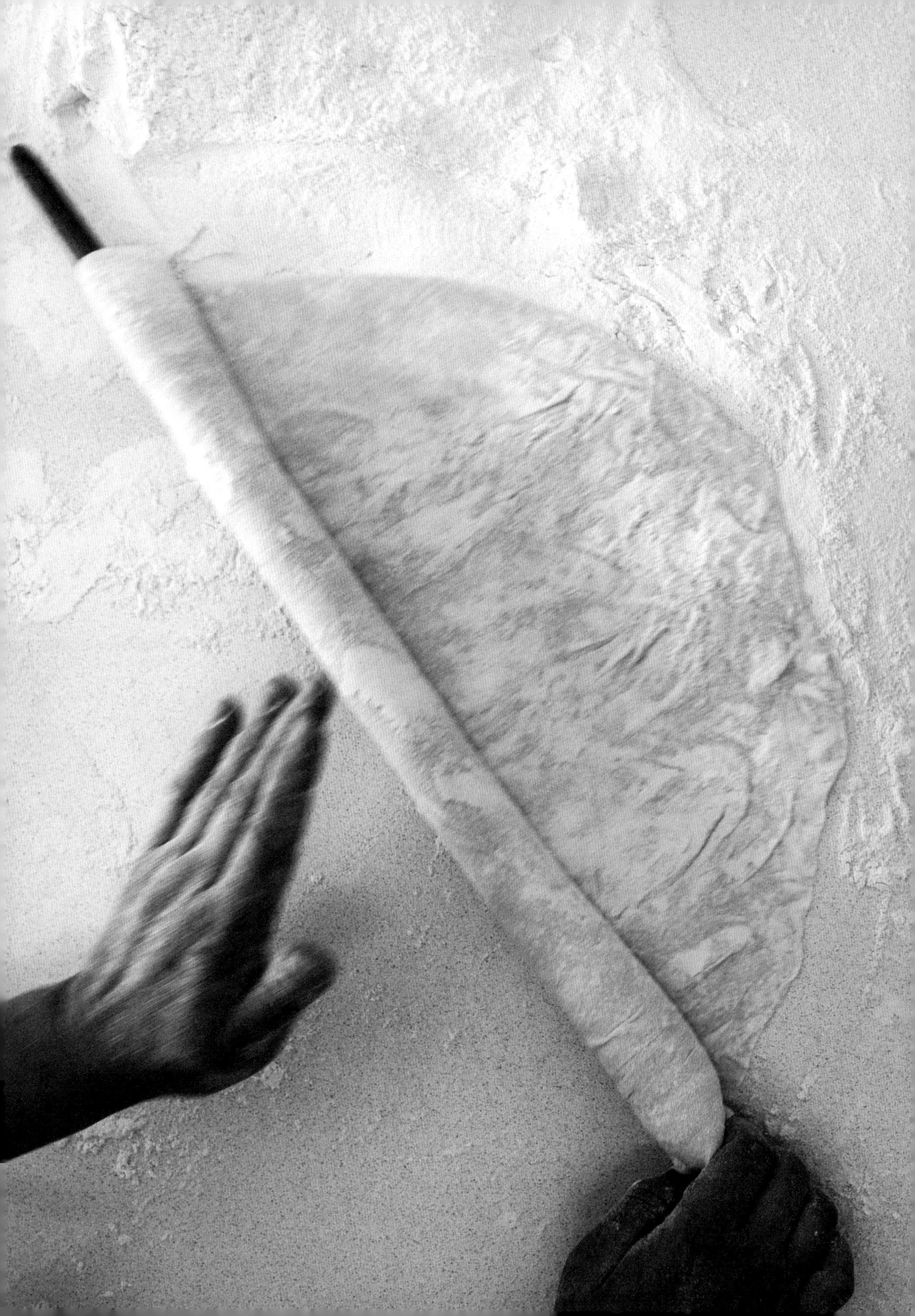

»Food must be affordable for everyone.«

officers during British rule. Our destination is Hagana Road 33 in the Hatikva Quarter, whose name can be translated as ›hope‹. At this point, it is difficult to imagine eating more food, but Kobi is unstoppable. He enthusiastically describes what's next: Dilek's. Dilek Bagci is a Turkish woman who makes the best filo dough in all of Tel Aviv. She does this in the traditional and labour-intensive manner in a tiny shop space on a street corner.

Kobi's appetite seems to be undiminished. We are immediately served platters of hot filo stuffed with spinach and cheese, accompanied by pickles and cream cheese. Kobi's enthusiasm is contagious: Dilek smiles modestly and offers us more Turkish specialties. On this non-descript street corner, a clientele consisting mostly of locals enjoys superb and authentic food for a few shekels. Now we are beginning to understand how Kobi selects his destinations.

Before we say our farewells, we ask Kobi what his favourite food is. Kobi surprises us with a rare moment of silent reflection and then says, ›The answer is kind of sad.‹ He thinks of his parents, both dead, and remembers *asida*, a dish from Tunis, the homeland of his grandfather. During his childhood, his parents often made this thick wheat pudding and usually served it with honey and butter. When we go our separate ways, not without making plans for future excursions in Kobi's Tel Aviv, he is back to his old self. He unpacks what he has brought with him in a paper bag from Dilek's shop, ready – as always – to try still more food and to share it with us.

In Haya's family, shakshuka is always served at Sunday brunch. A large pan of it is placed in the middle of the table and everyone dunks crisp bread into the sauce.

GREEN SHAKSHUKA

For 4–6 people for breakfast

- 100 g (3½ oz) leek
- 30 g (1 oz) butter
- 250 g (9 oz) spinach
- 25 g (1 oz) flat-leaf parsley
- 25 ml (¾ fl oz) cream
- Sea salt
- 1 small fennel bulb
- 2 spring onions (scallions)
- 1 tablespoon olive oil, plus extra for drizzling
- 50 g (1¾ oz) kashkaval, or another kind of mild, full-fat cheese
- 20 g (¾ oz) parmesan, plus extra to garnish
- 6 eggs
- Sourdough bread, to serve

Halve the leek lengthways, trim and cut into strips 1 cm (½ inch) wide. Melt the butter in a saucepan, add the leek and cook over medium heat until soft, about 15 minutes. Remove from the heat and let cool.

Wash spinach and remove the thick stems. Set aside about 50 g (1¾ oz) of the leaves. Blanch remaining spinach along with the parsley (with stems) for 10 seconds in boiling, salted water. Strain and immediately submerge in ice water. Firmly press to remove all liquid.

Purée the leek, spinach-parsley mixture, cream and 75 ml (2½ fl oz) of water with a stick blender or in a blender until creamy. Season to taste with salt.

Halve the fennel, remove the stalk and cut the bulb into thin slices. Trim the spring onions and cut in half widthways. Warm olive oil in a large frying pan over medium heat, add the spring onions and fennel and sauté very lightly for 3 minutes. Season with salt, transfer to a plate and set aside.

Add the remaining spinach and 1–2 tablespoons of water to the same pan. Sprinkle with salt and distribute first the spinach-parsley mixture and then the fennel and spring onions evenly over the spinach. Coarsely grate the kashkaval cheese and 20 g (¾ oz) parmesan and scatter over the vegetables. Using a spoon, make 6 small wells and break 1 egg into each. Salt well, especially the egg yolk, cover and cook for 4–5 minutes. The egg whites should be firm but the yolks still runny (like a poached egg).

Grate extra parmesan over the eggs. Drizzle with olive oil and serve with fresh sourdough bread.

HAYA'S TIPS:
IF YOU PREFER, YOU CAN ALSO MAKE THE SHAKSHUKA IN SMALL INDIVIDUAL PANS.

WE HAVE MADE COUNTLESS SHAKSHUKA VARIATIONS, INCLUDING A VERSION WITH CHICKPEAS AND EGGPLANT – WHATEVER TASTES GOOD IS ALLOWED! IT IS ALSO DELICIOUS AS LEFTOVERS.

VEGETARIAN SARMA

For 4–6 people as a main dish

For the filling:
- 250 g (9 oz) mushrooms
- 1 small carrot
- 1 small potato
- ¼ celeriac bulb
- ¼ kohlrabi
- 1 long red capsicum (pepper)
- 1 onion
- 1 tomato
- ½ teaspoon coriander seeds
- 2 sprigs dill
- 2 sprigs thyme
- ½ teaspoon black pepper
- 1 teaspoon paprika (sweet or hot, according to taste)
- 1 tablespoon sea salt
- 2½ tablespoons tomato paste (concentrated purée)
- 100 ml (3½ fl oz) canola oil
- 75 g (2½ oz) short-grain rice

- 100 ml (3½ fl oz) white vinegar
- 1 tablespoon sea salt
- 1 bay leaf
- 1 flat-head cabbage (Jaroma variety)

For the *filling,* clean and peel the mushrooms, carrot, potato, celeriac, kohlrabi, capsicum, onion and tomato as needed and coarsely grate or cut into very small cubes. Crush coriander seeds in a mortar. Finely chop the dill and pluck the thyme leaves from the stems. Place all ingredients except the rice in a large saucepan, cook for 10 minutes and then let cool for 15–20 minutes.

Meanwhile, bring the vinegar, salt and bay leaf to the boil in a large pan with enough water to cover the cabbage. Cut out the stem of the cabbage with a pointed knife. Place the cabbage head in the boiling water and cook for about 10 minutes, and then pull off the individual leaves. This is best done with a pair of tongs, removing the leaves one at a time while leaving the cabbage in the pan. You can also take the cabbage out of the water, let it cool briefly and then pull off the leaves.

Lay out the cabbage leaves flat on a chopping board and cut out the thick rib in the middle of each. Cut large leaves into three triangular pieces, smaller leaves into two.

Season the cooled vegetables to taste, then fold in the uncooked rice. Lay one cabbage leaf in the flat of your hand, put about 1 tablespoon of the vegetable filling on it and roll it up towards the tip – when it is filled, the leaf looks like a small ice-cream cone. Stick the overhanging piece of cabbage into the opening at the top and seal up the roll. Repeat this process until all the filling is used up. Shaping these rolls takes a bit of practice, but you will soon master it – and it is worth the trouble!

Cut the remaining cabbage into strips, lay in the bottom of a large, shallow saucepan and place the rolls tightly together on top. Pour in enough water to cover the sarma. Bring to the boil, cover and cook over low heat for about 1 hour. Serve hot or slightly warmed.

CREUSET

OKRA WITH LIMA BEAN CREAM

For 4 people as an appetiser

For the lima bean cream:

- 160 g (6 oz) lima beans (butter beans)
- 5 garlic cloves
- ½ small onion
- 2 sage leaves
- 70 g (2½ oz) unsweetened almond butter (from 100% almonds)
- ½ teaspoon sea salt

For the okra:

- 250 g (9 oz) okra
- 2 spring onions (scallions)
- 3 garlic cloves
- 2–3 slices pickled lemons (page 97)
- 1 acri sivri (cayenne) pepper
- 120 g (4¼ oz) grape tomatoes
- 6 tablespoons olive oil, plus extra to serve
- 1 handful coriander (cilantro) leaves
- 1 handful mint leaves
- Lime juice
- Sea salt

For the *lima bean cream*, place the beans in a bowl, cover with three times as much water and soak overnight.

The next day, strain the beans, place in a large saucepan and cover with water. Peel the garlic, peel and quarter the onion and add both to the pan along with the sage leaves. Bring to the boil and cook over low heat until the beans are soft and begin to fall apart, about 3 hours.

Strain the beans, saving the cooking water. With a stick blender or in a blender, purée the beans, onion and garlic together with the almond butter and salt, gradually adding a bit of cooking water to make a very smooth cream.

For the *okra*, remove the stem ends from the okra. Clean and trim the spring onions; cut the green parts into large pieces and finely dice the white parts. Peel the garlic and cut into thin slices. Finely dice the pickled lemons. Slice the sivri pepper into thin rings. Cut the tomatoes into wedges.

Heat olive oil in a frying pan over very high heat, add okra and white parts of the spring onions and sauté until the vegetables take on colour, 2–3 minutes. (Depending on the size of the pan, you might have to do this in more than one batch. The okra pods should just cover the bottom of the pan and not lie on top of each other. Then return all the vegetables to the pan.) Add the sivri pepper, garlic, tomatoes and pickled lemons and cook for 2–3 minutes.

Mix the coriander and mint leaves with 1 teaspoon lime juice and add to the vegetables with the green parts of the spring onions. Toss well and season to taste with salt and more lime juice.

Place the lima bean cream in a pan and gently reheat as necessary. If it is too thick, add a bit of water. Season to taste with lime juice and salt. Spread the lima bean cream on the plates and spoon the vegetables over the top. Drizzle with olive oil and serve.

ASIA
אסיה

THE COMMUNITY ORGANISERS

SHIRA PETEL & SHIRI ASSA

Shaffa

»The community organisers«

We have a date at the bustling Shuk Hapishpeshim, Jaffa's flea market, with Shira and Shiri, whose collaboration began with a small and very off-beat hair salon. Soon the salon developed into a social hub, and now the two partners operate several bars and restaurants on the newly popular Nakhman Street. With a great talent for communication and for disregarding conventions, they have created something refreshing and new in the old streets of Jaffa. This reminds us in a way of the beginnings of our NENI in Vienna: similar to us, Shira and Shiri opened their first business without much experience in the restaurant trade but armed with a great deal of vision, courage and passion – and it has continued to grow steadily in a very natural way.

The flea market is a popular spot on a Saturday morning, a bustling place perfect for finding a special bargain, for meeting a friend for coffee or just for meandering through the narrow streets of the old Arab quarter. This part of Jaffa used to be an area of old workshops, some of which still exist. Every afternoon the doors would close and the neighbourhood would grow quiet.

Recently Shira and Shiri put on their annual street party to celebrate Rosh Hashanah, the Jewish New Year. Some 150 workers helped set up, everyone brought food, a Turkish band played, and it was all free of charge. They recall with a laugh their first parties, at which Shiri's seven-year-old nephew served beer to the guests. Their street is a reflection of the evolution of this community and these changes present a difficult

reality. Once a predominantly Arab neighbourhood of local families who lived above the workshops and storefronts, it is now a trendy area attracting young Israelis. Shira and Shiri are conscious of these changes and respectful of what came before. Shaffa – the name of their company – comes from the Arabic verb ›to look‹ and is also Hebrew slang for a very good-looking girl. The logo in Hebrew and Arabic is stencilled, graffiti-style, on the outside wall of the Shaffa Bar. The tableware and much of the furniture are from the flea market; at first

glance the furnishings seem to have been chosen arbitrarily, but in fact they are often thought out down to the smallest detail.

Shira was born in Haifa to Iraqi parents. As a child, she refused to speak Arabic because she wanted to fit in. Today, Shira appreciates her Iraqi roots as being very much a part of her identity. Her parents, both university graduates, wanted her to find a successful career with a secure pension. Shira studied English literature and philosophy, taught English for several years at a special-education school and worked as the editor of a food company's website. The course of her life changed when she met Shiri.

Shiri was born in a moshav, a small rural workers' cooperative settlement. Her parents came from Bulgaria and Poland; along with Hebrew, the family spoke Bulgarian at home. When she first arrived in Jaffa, people referred to her as ›the Bulgarian‹. Shiri went on to study theatre and stage design to satisfy the career expectations her parents had for her. Shiri now laughs at their ominous warning when she was younger: ›If you don't study, you will end up in a hair salon.‹ Little did they know!

Shira and Shiri met over ten years ago through mutual friends. Both were married, with babies on the way. ›We liked hair styling and could handle scissors, but had no training in this profession.‹ Nevertheless, they spontaneously decided to team up and open a special kind of hair salon. They now say that at that time they gave birth not only to their children but also to a company. Today their business locations – similar to our NENI for us – are an extension of their home. Friends and family drop in just to say hello or to spend time together. The rapid and enormous success came as a complete surprise to both of them.

We are impressed by the lively and productive symbiosis between these two friends, by the free flow of ideas and stories from both of them. All business decisions are made jointly, and the close collaboration has not been detrimental to their friendship. Each has her own family and responsibilities. Shira lives with her husband and children in a residential part of northern Tel Aviv and for Shaffa focuses on food and writing. Shiri lives with her children and her partner in Jaffa and is responsible for design.

›At the beginning there was absolutely nothing here,‹ they say of their start on Nakhman Street. That was ten years ago. They just put two chairs on the sidewalk and cut hair out there. Fromthe very beginning it was not a conventional salon: they offered haircuts in exchange formusic performances, asked musicians to play Friday afternoons and evenings in front oftheir shop and sometimes even cut customers' hair outside during the concerts.

They expanded into the markets; they served coffee, sold second-hand clothing and began organising events ›for the fun of it‹. There was no business plan and no accountant. To this day, they operate more or less in the same spontaneous way – the two like to refer to themselves half-jokingly as ›non-businesswomen‹.

CROWN
Johnnie Walker

Memories of the foods of their childhoods and their love of all things culinary ultimately led them into the restaurant business. Shira recalls kibbeh with mushrooms and onions, and a spice mix called English Pepper. Her father and mother always cooked kibbeh together, making as many as 500 at a time and sending them as gifts to relatives as far off as London. Shiri, for her part, remembers thick slices of Polish-style bread with margarine, as well as an oven-baked sweet they called ›ice cream‹. It was not long before they began serving small samples of homemade food to their customers at the hair salon. One day someone told them that it was so good, it was worth paying for. And so the decision was born to expand into food, not for the sake of business but to expand the community idea.

»We want to do good, community-oriented things.«

›Why not open a café-restaurant?‹ they thought. And eight years ago that is exactly what they did, at a location a few doors from their salon. Haya has her hair cut here every time she visits; then she often meets friends and family at the café for a late breakfast, which flows seamlessly into a leisurely afternoon at the bar. One can easily spend an entire day seated here at one of the sidewalk tables.

Shaffa has never had any PR – word of mouth is more than sufficient. Shira and Shiri's business model appears to work: passion, resourcefulness, and wanting to ›do good, community-oriented things‹, rather than being motivated solely by profit. They both have a shared dream of moving out of the city to the vineyards and cultivating olive orchards. Perhaps they will open a guesthouse in the countryside or maybe a hospice where people could come to die in dignity surrounded by beauty. As always, they are open to future changes. ›Who knows what will come our way?‹ they say with a laugh.

LEEK BUNS

RECIPE FROM SHIRA PETEL AND SHIRI ASSA

For 4 buns

For the dough:
- O 80 g (2¾ oz) plain flour
- O 20 g (¾ oz) rice flour
- O 1 teaspoon dry yeast
- O ½ teaspoon baking powder
- O 1 teaspoon sugar
- O 60–70 ml (2-2¼ fl oz) tepid water
- O ½ teaspoon sea salt
- O 1 tablespoon canola oil, plus extra for working the dough
- O 1 egg yolk

For the filling:
- O ½ leek
- O 1 bunch chives
- O 2 tablespoons canola oil
- O Sea salt
- O Black pepper

For the dip:
- O 30 g (1 oz) fresh red chilli
- O 50 g (1¾ oz) garlic
- O 10 g (¼ oz) fresh ginger
- O 30 g (1 oz) sesame seeds
- O 2 teaspoons soy sauce
- O 2 teaspoons sesame oil
- O 250 ml (9 fl oz) grape seed oil

For the dough, use the dough hook of your stand mixer to slowly combine both flours, yeast, baking powder, sugar and water until you have a smooth dough, adding a bit more water as needed. Add the salt and oil and slowly knead for another 10 minutes. Cover and let rise at room temperature for 50 minutes. (You can also let the dough rise overnight in the refrigerator and bring it to room temperature before using it.)

While the dough rises, make the *filling*. Trim the leek and cut into thin strips; slice chives into thin rings. Warm the oil in a frying pan over medium heat, add the leek and slowly sauté. Stir in the chives and season to taste with salt and pepper. Leave to cool.

On a work surface brushed with oil, quarter the dough and shape into balls. Rub each ball well with oil and stretch into thin, round discs with your hands. Spread the filling evenly over the dough rounds, roll up each piece and shape into a snail. →

Bring a bit of water to the boil in a saucepan. Place the dough snails in a steamer basket or bamboo steamer and set in the pan. Cover and steam over simmering water for about 20 minutes, taking care that the dough does not touch the water but only steams.

Preheat oven to 240°C (475°F). Lay the steamed snails on a baking tray lined with baking paper, brush with the egg yolk and bake for 10–15 minutes in the oven. (You can also cook them in a pan with a bit of oil, frying them on both sides until golden brown.)

Meanwhile, make the *dip*. Halve the chillies lengthways and deseed. Peel the garlic and ginger. Dry-roast the sesame seeds in a pan. With a mortar or sharp knife, work the garlic, ginger and chilli together to make a paste. Stir in remaining ingredients.

Take buns out of the oven and serve, while still warm, with the dip.

HAYA'S TIP:
YOU CAN MAKE THESE BUNS WITH VARIOUS FILLINGS. I LIKE TO FRY CHICKEN MINCE WITH A BIT OF LEEK, GINGER AND CHILLI, SEASON IT WITH SOY SAUCE AND STUFF THE BUNS WITH THIS MIXTURE.

Place
MAKIAGE

ASIAN TROUT WITH CASHEWS

RECIPE FROM SHIRA PETEL AND SHIRI ASSA

For 4 people as a main dish

- O 40 g (1½ oz) cashews
- O 100 g (3½ oz) palm sugar (jaggery)
- O 50 ml (1½ fl oz) fish sauce
- O 50 g (1¾ oz) tamarind paste
- O Juice of 2 limes
- O 40 g (1½ oz) fresh ginger
- O 20 g (¾ oz) lemongrass
- O 20 g (¾ oz) fresh red chilli
- O 80 g (2¾ oz) shallots
- O 8 garlic cloves
- O 8 kaffir lime leaves
- O 2 untreated limes
- O 8 trout fillets, or branzino or sea bream
- O Tapioca flour, for dredging the fish
- O Canola oil, for deep-frying

HAYA'S TIPS:
IF YOU WANT TO IMPRESS YOUR GUESTS, ASK YOUR FISH SELLER TO CUT OPEN THE WHOLE TROUT LIKE A BUTTERFLY, AS IN THE PICTURE.

TAPIOCA FLOUR AND KAFFIR LIME LEAVES (FRESH OR FROZEN) ARE AVAILABLE AT ASIAN GROCERS.

THE CASHEWS CAN BE ROASTED A DAY AHEAD – OR YOU CAN FRY THEM UNTIL GOLDEN BROWN IN THE OIL LEFT FROM FRYING THE FISH.

Preheat the oven to 240°C (475°F) and roast the cashews on a baking tray lined with baking paper until golden brown, 7–9 minutes. Remove and allow them to cool completely (only then do they become crispy).

Slowly melt the sugar in a small saucepan and stir in the fish sauce, tamarind paste and lime juice.

Peel ginger and cut into thin strips. Remove the stem and tough outer leaves from the lemongrass and cut the inner part into thin slices. Cut chilli into rings; peel shallots and garlic and cut into very thin slices. Finely slice the kaffir lime leaves. Cut limes into thin slices and each slice into quarters. Mix everything together with the sauce and leave for at least 30 minutes.

Roll trout fillets on both sides in the tapioca flour, shaking off excess. Heat an ample amount of canola oil in a wide frying pan, add the fish and deep-fry.

Remove fish from the pan and arrange on plates or a serving platter, along with the Asian salad and the roasted cashews. Serve immediately.

MECHOUIA WITH ROCKET PESTO

HAYA'S TIP: THE VEGETABLES WILL KEEP FOR UP TO A WEEK IN THE REFRIGERATOR.

For 4 people as an appetiser

For the rocket pesto:

- O 50 g (1¾ oz) parmesan (Parmigiano Reggiano)
- O 6 garlic cloves
- O 25 g (1 oz) flat-leaf parsley
- O 30 g (1 oz) basil
- O 50 g (1¾ oz) rocket (arugula)
- O 50 g (1¾ oz) pine nuts
- O 3–4 tablespoons olive oil
- O ½ teaspoon salt
- O 1 tablespoon lemon juice

For the mechouia:

- O 1 onion
- O 1 large eggplant (aubergine)
- O 2 red capsicums (peppers)
- O 2 tomatoes
- O 1 spring onion (scallion)
- O 1 fresh red chilli
- O 1 acri sivri (cayenne) pepper
- O 2 garlic cloves
- O 5–6 tablespoons olive oil
- O Sea salt

- O 4 slices sourdough bread

For the *rocket pesto*, finely grate the parmesan and peel the garlic. Mix all ingredients in a blender or with a stick blender to make a smooth pesto.

For the *mechouia*, halve the onion. On a grill, char the eggplant, capsicums, tomatoes, spring onion, chilli, sivri pepper and onion on all sides. This can also be done under the oven's grill. (It is important that the vegetables are charred outside but very soft inside.) Peel while still hot and finely chop.

Peel and finely dice the garlic, and add to the vegetable mixture along with the olive oil. Season to taste with salt.

Toast the sourdough bread. Spread the chopped vegetables on the slices of bread and drizzle with the rocket pesto.

All that is necessary for this dish is top-quality vegetables and the correct preparation. It could hardly be easier or more delicious. Mechouia is especially suitable for a large group of guests: it can be served warm or at room temperature on a large platter

PANEER CURRY WITH PRUNES

For 4 people as a main dish

For the curry:

- O Canola oil for deep-frying, plus another 4 tablespoons of canola or grape seed oil for frying
- O 500 g (1 lb 2 oz) paneer cheese
- O 2 onions
- O 200 g (7 oz) pitted prunes
- O 2 cloves
- O 500 ml (17 fl oz) coconut milk
- O 75 g (2½ oz) tomato paste (concentrated purée)
- O 50 ml (1½ fl oz) maple syrup
- O ½ cinnamon stick
- O 1 teaspoon hot curry powder
- O ½ teaspoon chilli flakes
- O 1 pinch cayenne pepper
- O 1 tablespoon sea salt
- O 1 tablespoon flaked almonds
- O 1 tablespoon pepitas (pumpkin seeds)
- O 1 spring onion (scallion), green parts
- O 1 sprig coriander (cilantro)
- O Grated zest of 1 untreated lemon

For the rice:

- O 500 g (1 lb 2 oz) Japanese short-grain rice
- O 1 teaspoon sea salt

For the *curry,* heat an ample amount of canola oil in a tall saucepan. Cut paneer into 1 cm (½ inch) thick slices and then cut the slices into triangles. Deep-fry the cheese pieces in the hot oil until they have a golden-brown crust. Remove with a strainer and immediately place in a bowl of hot water. Let soak for 15 minutes. (This makes the paneer softer and gives it a nice consistency.) Then remove and drain.

While the paneer soaks, peel and finely chop the onions. Heat 4 tablespoons of canola oil in a frying pan, add the onions and sauté over medium heat for about 10 minutes.

Halve the prunes. Crush the cloves in a mortar. Add both, along with the coconut milk, tomato paste, maple syrup and the remaining seasonings, to the onions in the pan and simmer uncovered for 10–15 minutes.

Preheat oven to 190°C (375°F). Spread a bit of the prune sauce on the bottom of an ovenproof dish, place a layer of paneer on it and cover with sauce. Repeat this process until all the ingredients have been used up, finishing with a layer of sauce. Bake for 25 minutes in the oven. →

Wash *rice* in a sieve until the water runs almost clear. Bring to the boil with an equal amount of water, add salt, turn down the temperature to the lowest setting and cook for 10–15 minutes. Remove from the heat and leave to stand, covered, for 10 more minutes.

Meanwhile, dry-roast the almonds and pepitas in a small frying pan and coarsely chop. Trim the green parts of the spring onion and cut into very thin strips. Pluck the coriander leaves from the stems.

Remove the paneer curry from the oven and garnish with the almond-pumpkin seed mixture, spring onions, lemon zest and coriander. Serve rice separately.

HAYA'S TIPS:
YOU CAN REPLACE THE RICE IN THIS RECIPE WITH NAAN BREAD OR FLATBREAD.

THE PANEER CAN BE REPLACED WITH CHICKEN. WITH THE SWEETNESS OF THE PRUNES AND THE SLIGHT SPICINESS, THIS DISH IS THEN REMINISCENT OF MOROCCAN CUISINE.

TEDER
Valeria Monis
Shakar Marcus

THE MAGICIAN

ARIEL ROSENTHAL

HaKosem
»The Magician«

Ariel arrives at an outside table at his restaurant, cordial and attentive, aware of details. It is only mid-morning and already fried eggplant (aubergine), falafel, hummus, and a chickpea salad appear before us, followed by spicy potato slices and shakshuka. He declares: ›When you taste the food, you can understand me better.‹ Ariel is in his element in what has become a staple of Tel Aviv life – one of the most popular falafel places in the city and one of our regular destinations when we are here. People are already lining up to order or settling into the wooden tables out in front.

HaKosem is located on a busy street corner in central Tel Aviv. In the open kitchen behind the massive shawarma spit, food for the large number of customers is freshly prepared throughout the day: baba ganoush, falafel and nine batches of hummus daily! ›All over the world, good chefs are making street food,‹ says Ariel. For him, street food is a wonderful opportunity to express the unique feel of a place. ›This kind of food is full of life experience and memories, like a good song.‹ Many of the chefs we meet in Tel Aviv have a very philosophical attitude about what they do, and Ariel is no exception. He talks openly about his difficult childhood years, his adoption, about periods of living on the street, and years spent in Tel Aviv and Belgium without a stable home. The key to survival even back then was ›learning to hear, see, and smell everything very precisely‹. For him, the most important thing hasn't changed: understanding people.

The restaurant bears Ariel's nickname when he was a boy, HaKosem, Hebrew for ›the magician‹. The name comes from another childhood memory, a positive one. Close to where he lived when he was eight years old, there was a store selling magicians' supplies. He offered to help clean and keep the shop tidy, not for money, but in exchange for being taught magic tricks. He says, ›I became a magician because it fit my character.‹

Ariel's life in Tel Aviv improved after the difficult early years. He attended school, worked as a teenager at a supermarket, and then found a job at Café Zou. ›That was the best restaurant in Israel at the time,‹ he says proudly. He quickly gained experience as a waiter, at the bar, and then in the kitchen. Ariel sees this complete dedication to whatever he does as the key to his success. This energy and determination are written into the way he tells us his stories, provides us with food, directs his staff, and greets his customers – he is acutely aware of everything around him.

Now we are served a rice dish redolent with the fragrance of fried onion and sprinkled with juicy chickpeas. It is reminiscent of foods we know from other lands: *koshary* from Cairo, or rice with lentils from Morocco. Ariel laughs as he tells the story of this dish, which is now cooked daily just before the midday rush: One of his cooks was preparing the rice, as always with a base of fried onions. Ariel arrived at the restaurant and smelled that something had burned. The cook confessed that he had burned the onions at the bottom of the pot, and there was not enough time to make a new batch of rice. Ariel lifted the lid, tasted the rice, and found the slightly smoky taste delicious. A new recipe was born!

At age 26, after serving in the army, Ariel began studying to be a social worker. He thought about what it means to have a ›good life‹ and how he could feel good about his work and how he lives. ›One must know one's character but also be ready to change‹, is his motto. In his business, food, ingredients and the desires of the customers may all change, but ›what is really important is to stay true to oneself‹.

At the beginning of the new millennium, fast food in Tel Aviv consisted almost solely of falafel, hummus and shawarma. ›I can do that, too,‹ Ariel thought. His neighbourhood was expecting another falafel place with simple street food, but Ariel wanted more: cool furniture, nice plates, pleasant lighting, good music and top-quality ingredients. He wanted to offer not just falafel but the best falafel in the city. Through his love of detail and courage to break out of established boundaries, Ariel's restaurant reminds us of our NENI on Vienna's Naschmarkt – which is probably why we feel so at home here.

Ariel hopes that you feel the atmosphere of Tel Aviv here. We are impressed with his way of dealing with people. The cooks in the open kitchen and the service staff do their job jovially, efficiently and in a relaxed manner. ›The food must touch you,‹ he says. By the age of one, children in Israel are already eating the soft insides of a falafel and hummus and at an early age develop an emotional bond with these foods. Basically, he sees the food here as the result of ›taking a bit from everywhere and everyone and making it your own‹.

While we talk, Ariel does not miss a beat in his surroundings, always aware of the cooks behind the counter, the waitresses, guests coming in; he shakes hands, nods and waves at people passing in the street. He has established a large network, connects cooks with each other, and has no need for competitiveness. He is at home here and loves the area.

Nuriel had actually met Ariel in the neighbourhood long before our interview for this book. Not far from HaKosem is the former dentist's office of Haya's father, which has now been converted into an apartment for her entire Molcho family. One day, Nuriel and Ariel happened to both be in a nearby boutique when Ariel commented on Nuriel's unusual suit, which led to a chat about style, art and trends. On the first day of our interview when

»When you taste the food, you can understand me better.«

Nuriel wanted to take a picture of Ariel, he said, ›We can't do that today. Wait until tomorrow, then I'll put on a black T-shirt.‹ An encounter between two aesthetes!

Ariel is interested in fashion, finds Paris inspiring, and will travel to Riga the next day. He is also working on a cookbook – dedicated exclusively to one single food, but he won't tell us what it is. We're left in suspense. Shortly before our ›magician‹ leaves us, we ask him how he sees his future. He answers: ›Hopefully, still as a good life...in a humble way.‹

מסלול
איטי
SLOW LANE
השחייה
בצד
ימין
SWIM ON THE RIGHT SIDE
מסלול
בינוני
MIDDLING
LANE
השחייה
בצד
ימין
SWIM ON THE RIGHT SIDE

מסלול
מהיר
FAST LANE
השחייה
בצד
ימין
SWIM ON THE RIGHT SIDE
מסלול
מהיר
FAST LANE
מסלול
סנפירים
וכפות בלבד!
FINS LANE
ONLY!

The original version of messabecha is a warm, creamy hummus served with whole chickpeas. The messabecha made with white beans is a blend of two food traditions: white beans are a popular dish in Romania, made usually with onions and sage and always with plenty of garlic. Haya's father, who was a dentist in Israel, was once sent home from work by his boss for an entire week for eating too much garlic: the day before there had been messabecha for dinner. Since then, the family recipe has always been made without garlic.

WHITE-BEAN MESSABECHA

For 4–6 people as an appetiser

- O 400 g (14 oz) dried white beans
- O 2 small onions
- O 3 sprigs sage
- O 50 ml (1½ fl oz) olive oil, plus extra for drizzling
- O Sea salt
- O 1 tablespoon unhulled tahini
- O 1 tablespoon lemon juice
- O 1 acri sivri (cayenne) pepper
- O Challa (see page 253), to serve, or pita bread
- O Sumac, to garnish

Soak beans overnight in three times as much water as beans. The next day, pour through a strainer, wash under cold water and drain.

Peel onions. Bring beans to the boil in a large pan with 3 litres (105 fl oz) of water, onions, sage and olive oil, and cook for 1½ hours. Then add 1 tablespoon of salt and continue cooking until the beans are very soft, about 1 more hour. Add a bit more water as needed. When the beans are done, strain them, saving the cooking water, and allow to cool.

Using a blender or a stick blender, briefly whizz 420 g (15 oz) of the beans together with the tahini and lemon juice; small pieces should still be visible. Blend in a bit of cooking water as needed. Season to taste with salt.

Deseed the sivri pepper and finely dice. Toast the bread until dark brown. Spread the bean paste on plates. Arrange the remaining beans and the diced sivri on top, drizzle with olive oil and sprinkle with sumac. Serve with the bread.

HAYA'S TIP:
YOU CAN ALSO COOK THE BEANS IN A PRESSURE COOKER, WHICH REDUCES THE COOKING TIME TO 45 MINUTES.

THE URBAN FORAGER

HEELA HAREL

Artist and Recycler
»The Urban Forager«

Hunters and gatherers predate agricultural societies in human history. Today hunter-gatherers exist in only very few places in the world. Yet here, in the middle of the progressive, cosmopolitan city of Tel Aviv, we meet a modern-day, urban representative of this species: Heela Harel identifies and collects edible herbs and plants all over the city.

We meet her in the community garden that she was instrumental in setting up. Even in this dry season at the end of summer, the place is still lush with plants and flowers. A giant mural decorates one wall; scarecrows in the shape of women stand all over the garden like colourful sculptures. A mental health centre is across the street and a school is close by. Both facilities are involved in this community project established here among the bleak high-rise buildings. Heela exemplifies the optimism and spirit of this garden. She is creative and bursting with energy despite – or because of – the various roles she plays in her life: she is a graphic designer, fashion designer, artist and teacher. She has just recently taken a teaching job at the local primary school and, like all good teachers, wonders if she is fully prepared for this. This extraordinary woman tells us today about the city's edible secrets.

Heela's first question for us is: ›Are you really aware of all the things you can eat?‹ She doesn't wait for a response; in the same breath she tells us that she organises herb forays through the city. It is too dry for this now, but in spring, she says, one finds edible plants on every street corner, in front of every hedge and next to every bush. But here, in the irrigated community garden, there is still much to marvel at. We take a seat at a round table in the shade of a large tree. Heela tells us of her path through life, which – like that of so many people we have met in Tel Aviv – has not been exactly linear.

She was born in Jerusalem, where her parents still live, the second of six children in a very religious family. Heela's American mother has Ashkenazi roots and grew up on a farm in Connecticut, while her father is an Israeli of Kurdish heritage. Heela has fond memories of her mother often cooking with her, and the Iraqi-Kurdish foods of her father were also part of the family menu. Heela completed the first two grades of elementary school in the U.S., where she learned English for the first time. She quickly turned into a real bookworm and devoured all of her mother's English books. Later, when they had returned to Israel, Heela rebelled against her family: she refused to continue attending the religious school in a kibbutz near Jerusalem and wanted to switch to an art school. Her parents transferred her to another school, but not to the art school. Despite this difficult phase, she remained close to her family. Today Heela gives her parents credit for raising her to be someone who is unafraid of making her own decisions, and someone who stands up for her principles.

After her military service Heela worked with a theatre group, travelling to festivals in Copenhagen and New York. She wanted to become

»It's almost obscene to always buy new things.«

a producer and moved to Tel Aviv, where she gained experience in video studios and became a sought-after graphic designer. She is still highly successful in this profession and loves art of all kinds. She finds Tel Aviv to be a creative environment where people in the arts work with great dedication, but where they also easily burn out.

In 2001 Heela decided to fundamentally change her life. At the age of 29, she began studying to be a fashion designer at Shenkar College in Ramat Gan and became very involved in environmentalism and sustainability activism. Heela had always collected things, but now she became an outspoken advocate for recycling, even using a magnet to collect the lost sewing needles of other students. It seemed almost obscene to her to always buy new things and she wrote about fashion's link to second-hand clothes. Inspired by Shel Silverstein's poem 'Hector the Collector', she re-used jewellery, cut-up T-shirts and other found materials for her final art project at college. The result was both design-driven and very cheap, partly out of necessity and partly out of ideology.

As we talk, a friend of Heela's arrives at the garden to tend to some plants. She too is an artist who offers ceramics classes at the mental health centre across the street. Urban gardening is now in vogue everywhere, but its roots here in Tel Aviv go back a number of years. Heela moved to Florentin in 1997, an area that at the time was considered a slum. Before the present-day garden was established in 2014, another garden nearby had started as a grassroots project by locals, both as a meeting place and as an urban respite. Heela attended some of their community meetings and became a part of the group. Heela recalls a woman who never spoke with the others but always sat quietly on a bench and read. Only later did Heela find out that the silent woman was secretly bringing her compost from home and adding it to the soil of the garden. It served people in so many different ways.

Gradually, Heela assumed the leadership of the new community garden project. At the beginning, the present lot was barren ground, with the exception of a few lonely trees. Heela learned about organic gardening from the others, whom she describes as ›an easygoing group of strong individuals‹. There was no strict hierarchy, and plans evolved from one day to the next. Initially there were battles with the local government, but the project nonetheless turned into a success. ›The garden has a therapeutic effect on the entire community,‹ says Heela. Florentin has in the meantime become more fashionable but also much more expensive, and not all developments here have been positive. Heela hopes that, in any case, the local government will keep pace with all the community activism.

Her forays beyond the limits of the garden began when someone told her that you could eat dandelion leaves. She talks with great pleasure about how

incredible it was to realise just how much grows wild in the city: nettles, wild mustard, dandelions, berries and much more. On her constant search for new delicacies, Heela fearlessly samples nearly everything she can find: leaves, roots, bark and flowers. Now all of Tel Aviv has become her foraging territory. Heela is known here for her botanical tours of the city and even produces a live show called Wild Weeds.

Heela bends down and comes up with a handful of green leaves. She shows us the shape of the leaf and the colour of the stem; she tears off a piece, rubs it between her hands and lets us smell it. Its fragrance is a bit reminiscent of spinach, but fresher, somehow greener. She tells us that she finds as many as twenty different edible plants on a single afternoon, right by her front door. Some of them even have more nutrients than the food one buys at the supermarket.

Before we leave, Heela serves us delicious drinks made with collected herbs and an appetiser of green leaves and blossoms. As an artist, she finds it important that even these simple foods are beautifully arranged. With a smile, she confesses to us that some people call her the ›crazy herb witch‹. But it is much more frequent for someone to bring her a plant and ask, ›Can I eat this?‹

ROSE GERANIUM–BASIL SYRUP

RECIPE FROM HEELA HAREL

For about 500 ml (17 fl oz) of syrup

- 225 g (8 oz) sugar
- 480 ml (16 fl oz) water
- 1 handful of rose geranium leaves
- 6–7 basil leaves (Magic Mountain variety)
- Edible blossoms, to garnish

TIPS:

ROSE GERANIUMS AND MAGIC MOUNTAIN BASIL CAN OFTEN BE FOUND IN THE GARDENS AND PARKS OF TEL AVIV. THIS FRESH, FLOWERY SYRUP IS VERY AROMATIC AND IS DELICIOUS IN COCKTAILS OR ICE-COLD WHITE WINE. IT IS ALSO A GOOD SWEETENER FOR LEMONADE, FRUIT AND DESSERTS.

BY ALL MEANS USE WHITE SUGAR SO THAT THE BRIGHT GREEN COLOUR OF THE HERBS IS NOT DIMINISHED.

IT CAN HAPPEN THAT THE INDIVIDUAL COMPONENTS OF THE SYRUP SEPARATE AFTER A WHILE, SO ALWAYS SHAKE WELL BEFORE SERVING.

Blitz all ingredients for 30 seconds in a blender or with a stick blender to completely dissolve the sugar. Let mixture steep for several hours or overnight.

The next day, strain the liquid through a tea towel to remove all plant parts. Pour into bottles and place in the refrigerator. Syrup will keep for several days if well chilled.

Dilute with sparkling water and garnish with blossoms.

SABICH

For 4–6 people for any time of the day or night

For the tomato salad:
- O 4 tomatoes
- O 1 garlic clove
- O 1 handful coriander (cilantro) leaves
- O 2 tablespoons olive oil
- O 1 teaspoon lemon juice
- O Sea salt

For the eggplant:
- O Canola oil, for deep-frying
- O 2 eggplant (aubergines)
- O Plain flour, for dusting
- O Sea salt

- O 5 eggs
- O Sea salt
- O 4–6 small, round pieces of focaccia bread (page 93)
- O 250 g (9 oz) tahini (page 94)
- O 80 g (2¾ oz) amba (page 94)
- O 50 g (1¾ oz) zhug (page 95)
- O 1 handful coriander (cilantro) leaves

For the *tomato salad,* dice the tomatoes, and peel and finely chop the garlic. Finely chop the coriander leaves as well. Mix the garlic and coriander together with the olive oil and lemon juice in a bowl and season with salt. Fold in the diced tomatoes and leave until you are ready to serve.

Heat an ample amount of canola oil in a deep saucepan. Peel the *eggplant* and cut lengthways into 5 mm (¼ inch) thick slices. Dust with flour and fry in the hot oil until they take on a golden-brown colour. Remove with a mesh strainer, drain on paper towels and season with salt.

Boil the eggs for 6½ minutes, then peel, cut in half or into slices and season with salt. Drizzle the focaccia with tahini and amba. Distribute the eggplant, eggs and tomato salad over the top, season with zhug and garnish with coriander leaves.

HAYA'S TIPS:
IF YOU LIKE, YOU CAN ALSO SLICE THE FOCACCIA OPEN AND STUFF THEM INSTEAD OF PUTTING EVERYTHING ON TOP.
EACH FLAVOUR COMPONENT IS IMPORTANT, SO DON'T OMIT ANY ELEMENTS OF THIS DISH, EVEN IF IT IS A BIT OF WORK. IT IS THE COMBINATION OF ALL THE INGREDIENTS THAT MAKES THE SABICH SO SUPERB.

If there is a dish that symbolises the flavour of Tel Aviv, then it is sabich. Every time Haya visits the city, the first trip she makes is to a sabich stand.

This sandwich takes its name from its inventor: Sabich Tsvi Halabi – a Jew who originally came from Iraq – was the first to have the idea of combining the boiled brown eggs left over from the cholent served on Shabbat with the ingredients of a classic Iraqi-Jewish breakfast. He sold his new creation from a small shack near a bus terminal, and his first customers were primarily bus drivers. This sandwich soon soared in popularity, with new sabich stands opening constantly. Today the sabich is among the few foods that were truly created in Israel.

NENI'S BASIC COMPONENTS

WHAT WE ALWAYS HAVE AT HOME

FOCACCIA

For 1 large or 6 small loaves of bread

- O 500 g (1 lb 2 oz) plain flour, plus extra for the work surface
- O 20 g (¾ oz) sugar
- O 10 g (¼ oz) sea salt
- O 5 g (⅛ oz) dry yeast
- O 25 ml (¾ fl oz) olive oil, plus oil for the baking sheet
- O 340 ml (11½ oz) water
- O Coarse sea salt, for sprinkling the dough

Mix the flour, sugar, salt and yeast in a bowl. Add the olive oil and water and knead by hand or using a stand mixer with a dough hook until you have a sticky dough. Cover the bowl with plastic wrap, puncture twice with a fork and let the dough rise for 12–24 hours in the refrigerator.

Use the risen dough for 1 large loaf of bread or divide into 6 portions. For a large focaccia, dust the dough in the bowl with flour and then turn onto your work surface with the floured side down. Fold the edges of the dough to the middle all the way around and press firmly, always rotating the ball of dough a bit. Then turn so that the smooth side is up. For small loaves, roll the bits of dough with your cupped hand on an unfloured surface to shape them into balls. Cover dough and let rest for 30 minutes at room temperature. Preheat oven to 260°C (500°F).

Brush a baking tray with olive oil. With oiled hands, carefully stretch the large ball of dough over the entire baking tray and press flat; shape the small balls into round flatbreads. With spread fingers, make indentations in the surface of the dough and sprinkle with coarse sea salt. Bake until the focaccia is golden brown, about 10–12 minutes. Bake the small portions for 5–6 minutes, doing this in two batches if they do not all fit on a baking tray. Let the focaccia cool a bit before serving.

The whole world meets in Tel Aviv, which is also reflected in the city's kitchens – especially when it comes to bread. Focaccia was brought to Israel by Italian Jews, and sourdough bread from San Francisco has followed in the past fifteen years. These kinds of culinary ›newcomers‹ are combined with familiar foods, resulting in a steady stream of new and exciting dishes.

AMBA

For about 500 g (1 lb 2 oz)
- O 300 g (10½ oz) mango pickles
- O 100 ml (3½ fl oz) water
- O 100 ml (3½ fl oz) canola oil

Mix all ingredients in a blender or with a stick blender until you have a very smooth, creamy sauce.

HAYA'S TIPS:
A VARIETY OF MANGO PICKLES CAN GENERALLY BE FOUND AT INDIAN AND ORIENTAL SUPERMARKETS. WE USUALLY USE A MEDIUM-HOT PRODUCT WITH LARGE, GOLDEN-YELLOW CHUNKS OF MANGO.

THE SAUCE WILL EASILY KEEP FOR THREE WEEKS IN THE REFRIGERATOR AND GOES WELL NOT ONLY WITH SABICH BUT ALSO WITH SOUPS AND LENTIL DISHES.

Large bottles of amba stand on the tables of every sabich stand in Tel Aviv. Guests can use as much or as little as they like.

TAHINI

For about 150 g (5½ oz)
- O 1 tablespoon lemon juice
- O ½ teaspoon sea salt
- O 140 g (5 oz) unhulled tahini

Stir the lemon juice, salt and 110 ml (3½ fl oz) of water together in a tall container. Gradually work in the tahini with a whisk or a stick blender until everything is well blended and the tahini is smooth and creamy.

HAYA'S TIPS:
IN ISRAEL, BOTH THE PURE SESAME PASTE AND THE SAUCE MADE FROM IT ARE CALLED TAHINI, SO ALWAYS CHECK THE INGREDIENTS LIST BEFORE YOU BUY.

IF YOU LIKE, YOU CAN VARY THE SAUCE WITH FINELY CHOPPED GARLIC, COOKED RED BEETROOT OR BLANCHED AND PURÉED HERBS. THE DIFFERENT VERSIONS MAKE FOR A VARIETY OF FLAVOURS AND APPEARANCES.

Haya searched for a long time for the right tahini producer. When she ate the best tahini of her life at a restaurant in Israel, she asked the owner about the source. The tahini, he said, came from a Samaritan family who lived on the sacred Mount Gerizim in Palestine. Because of the occupation, visiting there was dangerous, especially for women. Neither the restaurant owner nor any taxi driver wanted to take Haya to Mount Gerizim, and all warned her not to go. But Haya was persistent, and finally a young taxi driver who desperately needed money took her there. She had done what no one thought was possible. Today NENI is the largest purchaser of this producer's tahini – the Samaritan family has now built a second factory to keep up with demand.

ZHUG

For about 100 g (3½ oz)
- O 3 garlic cloves
- O 15 g (½ oz) coriander (cilantro)
- O 25 g (1 oz) parsley
- O 2 acri sivri (cayenne) peppers
- O 4 tablespoons olive oil
- O Sea salt

Peel garlic and chop very finely. Cut off the bottom part of the herb sprigs. Chop the coriander and parsley very finely. Deseed the sivri pepper and chop very finely. You can also coarsely chop everything and put it through a meat grinder or coarsely purée it in a blender (leaving some pieces whole).

Combine the mixture with olive oil, and salt to taste.

In Yemen, herbs are used a great deal in cooking, and spicy food is very popular. Zhug is the logical combination of both. This spicy herb paste is eaten there with vegetables, fish, meat, bread and hummus. It goes well with just about everything and frequently adds the finishing touch to a dish.

HARISSA

For about 700 g (1 lb 9 oz)
- O 200 g (7 oz) dried red pointed peppers
- O 100 g (3½ oz) dried hot red chillies
- O 8 garlic cloves
- O 50 g (1¾ oz) coriander (cilantro) (with the stems)
- O 20 g (¾ oz) sea salt,plus extra to season
- O 20 g (¾ oz) sugar
- O 300 ml (10½ fl oz) olive oil

Bring 5 litres (170 fl oz) of water to the boil in a large saucepan. Remove from the heat and add the pointed peppers and chillies. Cover with baking paper and weigh down with a plate so the chillies are completely covered with water. Leave for 1 hour.

Remove the chillies from the water and drain. Peel the garlic. Work all ingredients into a paste using a stick blender, blender or meat grinder, and salt to taste.

HAYA'S TIP:
I ALWAYS MAKE A LARGE AMOUNT OF HARISSA. STORED IN CANNING JARS AND COVERED WITH OLIVE OIL, IT WILL KEEP IN THE REFRIGERATOR FOR UP TO A YEAR AND IS ALWAYS PERFECT FOR GIVING A DISH THE NECESSARY >BITE<. IT IS ALSO A GOOD BASE FOR MARINADES. TO MAKE A SMALLER AMOUNT, SIMPLY HALVE THE RECIPE.

Even though pickled lemons are found in many culinary traditions, their roots are in Morocco. Here, salted lemons are ubiquitous and can be found in many dishes. Haya once returned to Vienna from a trip to India with tiny lemons bursting with juice and pickled them as the Moroccans do. That is true fusion cuisine!

PICKLED LEMONS

For 2 canning jars

- O 10 untreated lemons (approx. 500 g/1 lb 1 oz)
- O 100 g (3½ oz) sea salt
- O 50 g (1¾ oz) sugar
- O Olive oil

Cut lemons into slices about 1.5 cm (⅝ inch) thick and discard the ends. In a large bowl, mix the lemon slices with the salt and sugar. Let rest at room temperature for 48 hours, stirring twice a day. Rinse out canning jars with boiling water. Pack the lemon slices tightly in the jars, adding any liquid left in the bowl. Add enough olive oil to the jars to completely cover the lemons, seal and shake well. Leave at room temperature for two weeks, occasionally turning the jars over. Leave to rest in the refrigerator for another two weeks. Then the pickled lemons are ready to use.

HAYA'S TIPS:
THE PICKLED LEMONS KEEP NEARLY INDEFINITELY. TAKE THEM OUT OF THE REFRIGERATOR IN ADVANCE SO THE OIL CAN REACH ROOM TEMPERATURE.

TAKE CARE TO PRESERVE THE LEMONS IN SEASON, WHEN THEY ARE STILL FULL OF JUICE. YOU CAN ALSO PICKLE THEM WHOLE, IN WHICH CASE YOU SHOULD USE THE SMALLEST LEMONS YOU CAN FIND AND CUT A CROSS IN THE BASE OF EACH ONE BEFORE MARINATING. THEY SHOULD HAVE AS THIN A RIND AS POSSIBLE.

IF YOU ARE COOKING NENI STYLE, MAKE SURE YOU ALWAYS HAVE A SUPPLY OF PICKLED LEMONS ON HAND. WE SERVE THEM WITH FISH, MIX THEM INTO SALADS AND USE THEM TO GIVE STEWS AND SAUCES THE FINISHING TOUCH.

LEMON PESTO

For a simple lemon pesto, purée 200 g (7 oz) pickled lemons, mix in 120 ml (3¾ fl oz) olive oil and 45 g (1½ oz) harissa and season it with a bit of salt. The pesto keeps in the refrigerator for several weeks. It goes well with grilled fish and meat.

THE TRENDSETTERS

הרודן משתעשע
מוסא חלאלה
BORDELLO
A PARIGI
MICHA TV

PORT SAID / TEDER GROUP

Zach Bar

»The Trendsetters«

A non-descript building that once housed a shopping mall, across from the city's largest synagogue, is now home to one of the most exciting and popular meeting places in Tel Aviv. Originally the location for a one-off pop-up festival for only 100 days, Port Said restaurant is part of an initiative that now consists of a radio station, bars, restaurants and a dizzying number of events and projects. Whenever Nuriel steps off the plane in Tel Aviv, Port Said is always his first destination. We meet Zach Bar at the lively restaurant and sit at an outside table. When all the tables are taken, the next guests simply grab a free chair and have a seat on the sidewalk. A huge portrait of the Egyptian singer Farid al-Atrash looks down at the cheerful assembly. Music is the pulse of this restaurant; it is present constantly and everywhere.

Zach is one of four founding partners of the Teder Group, which operates all of the locations. He will describe for us today the long and not always linear path that has led to the present company, which now has some 300 employees. Zach's story comes in instalments as he frequently jumps up to greet a friend or guest. His abundance of energy is palpable. He tells us that, for him, this place is the ›real Tel Aviv‹ – for people of all ages and backgrounds who just want to enjoy music, a beer and some tahini. He loves it here: ›It is my home,‹ he says, ›and we have remained faithful to our original goals.‹

Zach has always had a passion for music. With his Turkish and Romanian roots, he has always been interested in music from different cultures. Very early in life, he began collecting and listening to a wide range of musical genres. As a teenager, he spent time in London, which, as he says, ›opened my mind.‹ He also visited Turkey, Greece and the U.S. After serving in the army, he lived in New York from 1999 to 2002, where he found an office job. But after the attacks of 9/11 his visa application was suspended, so he returned to Tel Aviv, of which he today says: ›Tel Aviv was always a wannabe city, wanting to be like New York, like Berlin, like Barcelona. It is small but still gives an indication of what a metropolis can be.‹ He had always loved the nightlife of Tel Aviv.

Back home, Zach tried to figure out what direction his life should take. He moved to Florentin and began working as a DJ in this up-and-coming neighbourhood. Before long, he joined a new radio station, 106 Fm Kol HaCampus, which was operated by students from the University of Tel Aviv. There he was responsible for selecting the music for the weekly radio show. The station became a platform for quality music, where artists, creative minds, and students ›worked together as one happy family‹, as Zach recalls.

Zach then became the manager of an unusual jazz band, The Apples, producing their first album and accompanying them on a five-year tour through Europe. Until 2012 he managed artists, organised music events in Israel and abroad and developed a large network. He sees the music industry as a colourful melting pot ideal for trying out ideas, ›inspired by the outside world while being connected to what you have here‹. He finds the same appeal in Tel Aviv, a city as an ›anchor with so many echoes to the outside‹. On the record label he had started in 2011, Fortuna Records, Zach released old albums of music he calls ›East meets West‹, including music popular in Israel in the early days of the country. His label helped old-school Arabic music to become more recognised here.

In 2010, Zach met his present partners, Shlomi Zidane, Dror Sher and Itai Drai, with whom he started an internet-based radio station, initially just a platform for their friends. Zach recalls the initial hectic period of experimentation, and a kind of out-of-the-box thinking that he and his partners still retain today. In the summer of 2010, they held a pop-up festival that was a huge success and broke the ›glass wall‹ between the radio studio and the audience once and for all. Over 3,000 people gathered on the street and partied together. As the demand for live events grew, a ›radio bar‹ was created in addition to what was now an annual festival and installed at the location that now houses their restaurant, Port Said.

Food was the next step in this development. ›Our DNA was always about people, music, food and drinks and the connection between them all,‹ says Zach. Teder had already collaborated with Eyal Shani, the famous Israeli chef and restaurateur, at their second festival. In 2012, they joined forces to open Port Said, which has become one of the most successful restaurants in the city. This place has a very special meaning for Elihay as well: he was offered his first position as head chef here when he was only eighteen; he worked at Port Said for two years and helped make it a well-known restaurant. We enjoy a glass of rosé and some spicy green beans and admire the atmosphere. The high walls are lined with vinyl records to the ceiling like books in a library. There is no mixing of music, only one record player. Their philosophical approach was to keep it simple. Every time the music changes, the cover of the new album is displayed above the DJ stand for all to see. Many of the artists are still little known and new discoveries for us as well. We make note of some of the names so that we can later compile our own Tel Aviv soundtrack.

Teder continued to develop and began expanding internationally. At some point, ›the whole world was calling‹, as Zach puts it. In 2012 they spent three weeks in Japan with a pop-up project: Teder Tokyo was sponsored by the Israeli Ministry of Foreign Affairs as a cultural exchange, and forty Teder people went to Japan to make it happen. Teder pop-ups in St Petersburg and Krakow followed, and now another one is planned for Paris.

The group also wanted to create something permanent in Tel Aviv, envisioning a multi-disciplinary space, an urban museum, a cultural centre, as well as a space for an open-air cinema, fashion shows and concerts. In 2013 they finally found the ideal location: Beit Romano on Jaffa Street. Eyal Shani again took charge of all the food; his Beit Romano restaurant is upstairs and a pizzeria is on the ground floor. They host over 200 events per year, and thanks to institutional and commercial support, they do not charge admission. We experienced the upbeat, lively mood of an old-fashioned fun fair there during Rosh Hashanah, with people dancing to live music and playing games. Zach is aware that the area of Beit Romano is becoming ›gentrified‹ and admits that Teder are in part responsible for this. He says that they are a pioneering force in the city, but that they have tried to ›move in‹ in a considerate way.

As we sit at Port Said – bar, restaurant and radio station – enjoying great food, listening to good music and taking in the buzzing atmosphere, it is obvious to us that the trendsetters of Teder have found innovative ways to bring people together and make them happy.

»Our DNA was always about people, music, food and drinks and the connection between them all.«

320

PORT
SA'ID

THE FOOD WRITER

RONIT VERED

Haaretz
»The Food Writer«

Ronit suggests that we meet at Hanan Margilan, a small, family-run Bukharan restaurant. With its unassuming atmosphere, it seems a surprising choice from a well-known food journalist. However, as Ronit greets us, she immediately announces that this is one of her favourite places to eat in Tel Aviv, and it is clear from the welcome she receives in the kitchen that she is a regular here.

Ronit is the author of several books and has been writing for Haaretz, one of Israel's most important newspapers, for over ten years. Her food topics are as diverse as the country itself: culinary history, eating customs, travel, anthropology and cultural history. We look forward to getting her perspectives on many aspects of food in this city and country. Ronit begins with the honest admission (like so many other people we have met here): ›We don't really know what Israeli food is.‹

Ronit has lived in Tel Aviv for twenty years but grew up north of the city on a moshav, a workers' cooperative settlement similar to a kibbutz. As a third-generation Israeli, with Romanian and Ukrainian roots, Ronit has developed an interesting theory about the generational changes in Israel and their impact. The first generation was busy just trying to survive, the second was not very interested in its cultural background, but now the third generation has the chance to focus on its roots again. Ronit senses, all around, a renewed interest in cultural origins and culinary authenticity. Even our meeting place exemplifies two important food influences often at work here in Tel Aviv: the local one and the communities of the Diaspora. It is a family-run Bukharan establishment that has made itself at home here. Ronit notes that this ›return to the roots‹ also contributes to a move away from the industrial food that has become so widespread today.

Identity in Israel is always complex; thus, Ronit often refers to anthropology, sociology, and history in order to try to better understand and explain it. She sees Tel Aviv as the only truly suitable place for secular people to live in Israel, which is why this city – in contrast to Jerusalem – has become the centre for new cultural and culinary trends. This city brings new traditions into the midst of this complex region and is also a place for improvising and trying new things. As a strong critic of Israeli policies, she sometimes thinks of leaving Israel, but she says that Tel Aviv is the only place where a lot of people think like her, people who believe that Palestinians should have more rights. This is also why she lives in this city.

Many influences on what is today known as ›Israeli cuisine‹ come from different Arab cuisines that existed here long before the founding of Israel. Outside influences were added with the influx of Jews from other countries. But not all immigrant groups have had an equal impact on these food traditions. North African cooking, particularly Moroccan and Tunisian, and Iraqi cuisine have left a distinctive mark. While Turkish cuisine had a pronounced influence on the region during the Ottoman period, Persian food – which greatly shaped the Arab style of cooking in Europe – played a less significant role, with none of their dishes having become part of the Israeli cooking canon. Eastern European culinary traditions of the Ashkenazi also do not represent an important part of the new Israeli food culture; they have the reputation of being something only for the ›old Jews‹, with little colour and taste. However, a few ›classic‹ dishes of this cuisine from the Diaspora remain, such as challa and cholent. These foods can be cooked before the Shabbat, when very devout Jews are not allowed to make a fire.

»Food always transcends cultural borders.«

In this way, some foods that come from religious traditions are common to all Israelis.

›Food always transcends cultural borders,‹ says Ronit, who finds that this is the beauty of it; attempts to define foods by ›national‹ borders, on the other hand, are counterproductive. Before the artificial borders in this region were created, there was a constant exchange among the people who lived here, and it was not important who created what first.

From 1995 to 2005, there were many popular haute cuisine restaurants in Tel Aviv. Although almost all have since closed down, they continue to play a major part in Israel's constantly changing restaurant scene. The boom of the Israeli ›food revolution‹ began with Haim Cohen's famous restaurant Keren. He was the first to combine local ingredients with French haute cuisine, experimenting with sophisticated techniques and drawing on recipes from his grandmother. Eyal Shani, the owner of Abraxas and Miznon as well as the culinary mastermind behind the Teder Group (page 102), also contributed to this change with an original approach to the Israeli restaurant culture. This all became part of the language of a new Israeli cuisine, which Ronit says is easier to define abroad. It is now known as daring, varied, and improvisational, with an emphasis on fresh vegetables and fruit. It also takes much from the local Palestinian cuisine from which ›street food‹ came up with the idea ›Put it in a pita‹.

In her column ›Pleasure Hunting‹, Ronit tries to avoid making judgments; she simply wants to tell stories, to ›describe reality as it exists‹. She rarely writes about celebrity chefs; she is more interested in subjects like the efforts to bring back ancient varieties of wheat that are no longer grown here. Or sesame, which grew in this region for over 5,000 years before it almost completely disappeared from Israel as an agricultural crop. In the 1960s and '70s, both Jews and Arabs tried to cultivate sesame here more extensively but it continues to be largely imported from Ethiopia because it is time-consuming, and thus expensive, to cultivate. An animated ode to tahini ensues, which leads Ronit to the subject of hummus. ›The best hummus is not to be found in restaurants,‹ she declares. ›The best hummus is made at home.‹

In her concern for Palestinian rights, Ronit writes a great deal about Palestinian cuisine and the everyday difficulties faced by the Palestinians here. She tells us about the problems of two cooks from Gaza who used to work at Keren but because of political tensions have been excluded from the Tel Aviv restaurant scene. But there are some positive initiatives, as well, such as Marimati at the Shuk Hapishpishim, the flea market in Jaffa. There, a mother and son serve Arab food, and it is again the same process: the third generation creating something new by going back to the roots. Equally successful is the collaboration between a Jewish Israeli and an Arab Israeli who jointly opened an ice cream parlour called Buza (meaning ›ice cream‹ in Arabic), which has now made a name for itself in the city.

When it comes to food, Ronit is a walking encyclopaedia. She has recently written essays for the cookbook *Divine Food*, and she highly recommends that we watch the film *The Search for Israeli Cuisine*. From the great flood of information, new discoveries and traditions, she always selects her topics according to one criterion: ›I like to write about people who are passionate about what they do.‹

eurolux 50W

VEGETABLE BROTH

For about 3 litres (105 fl oz)

- O 2 large onions
- O 1 leek
- O 2 carrots
- O ½ celeriac
- O 5 celery stalks
- O 2 parsley roots

HAYA'S TIP:
THE COOKING TIME FOR THE BROTH CAN VARY. AN EASY WAY TO TEST IF IT IS READY IS TO TRY A PIECE OF VEGETABLE: IF IT TASTES LIKE NOTHING, THEN ITS ENTIRE FLAVOUR HAS GONE INTO THE BROTH, WHICH IS NOW READY TO USE.

Peel vegetables as needed and cut into 1 cm (½ inch) dice. Place in a large saucepan along with 4 litres (140 fl oz) of water, bring to the boil and simmer for about 1 hour over medium heat. Strain the broth into large jars while it is still warm, and then seal tightly.

The broth will keep in the refrigerator for 4 to 5 days. It can also be frozen.

CHICKEN BROTH

For about 3 litres (105 fl oz)

- O 2 large onions
- O 1 leek
- O 2 carrots
- O ½ celeriac
- O 5 celery stalks
- O 2 parsley roots
- O 2 chicken legs or 750 g (1 lb 10 oz chicken bones

Peel vegetables as needed and cut into 1 cm (½ inch) dice. Cut chicken legs along the bone and pull the meat apart slightly. Place everything in a large saucepan along with 4 litres (140 fl oz) of water, bring to the boil and simmer for about 1 hour over medium heat. Strain the broth into large jars while still warm, and then seal tightly.

The broth will keep in the refrigerator for 4 to 5 days. It can also be frozen.

THE PURIST

FDNY
FIRE DEPT.

ASAF DOKTOR

Dok
»The Purist«

»Dok is a never-ending project.«

On bustling Ibn Gabirol Street – named after the 11th-century Andalusian poet and Jewish philosopher Solomon Ibn Gabirol – we meet Asaf in his small restaurant, Dok, which opens directly onto the street promenade. Fresh Israeli herbs in clay pots signal the important role of locally grown food, while the aesthetic of the restaurant is reflected in the neatly arranged and beautifully wrapped cakes and jam jars on shelves along the walls. Out on the sidewalk, herbs wind their way up a column, a small vertical garden in the middle of the city. We are here on the afternoon before the Jewish New Year. Usually serving meals only in the evening, Dok has organised something special for the occasion. The place is busy; on the counter are small samples for customers to taste as they wait in line to take cookies, fruit pastes and marzipan home for the holiday. Warm, crispy slices of a delicious lemon tart are brought directly from the kitchen for us to try.

Everything served in this restaurant – literally every single item – is made with local ingredients. That is the foundation of Dok's raison d'etre. Hence, there is no chocolate and no black pepper. When we accept the offer of coffee, Asaf brings it to us from the place next door. Whatever they make, serve and sell here comes from Israel. Asaf had to overcome many difficulties before he was able to achieve this vital example of a low carbon footprint. He sits down with us and opens up, with a sense of bemusement, about his successes, failures and learning experiences on the path to what has now proven to be a successful concept.

Asaf tells us about his Austrian grand-parents, from whom he has his family name. It is also the origin of the restaurant's name, in abbreviated form. Asaf was born in Caesarea to an architect and designer mother whose influence is evident here in Dok's design. His father is an aeroplane mechanic and Asaf's brother Yotam is a business partner. Asaf started cooking at age 16, worked himself up from a kitchen assistant, and eventually took cooking classes. He always liked cooking for friends and playing the host. He always wanted to be a chef, driven by his love of food. He eventually learned a great deal at the famous Orca restaurant and became sous-chef at Helena, in Caesarea harbour. After spending some time in London, he decided to go into business for himself – focusing on something besides ›fine dining‹.

Asaf reflects on the rich experience of what did and did not work before opening Dok and he identifies stubbornness as a necessary quality in Tel Aviv's restaurant business. At Tapeon, a tapas bar in Tel Aviv that specialised in raw food, he had an idea. In what is now the location of Dok, he and three partners got together eleven years ago and launched Carpaccio Bar, a raw food restaurant. The orientation was international and modern: it offered gazpacho, ceviche and carpaccio. Asaf felt right at home in the small restaurant, but he still recalls the difficult beginnings with few customers. With that certain stubbornness and a great deal of perseverance, the bar eventually succeeded and survived for eight years. Today he dismissively refers to the whole endeavour as a ›shitty idea‹. So, on to the next one! They opened an old-school grill place – the complete opposite of the raw food concept – and hoped for better success; however, it was not profitable, they didn't yet know much about efficient management, and the food, by Asaf's own admission, was ›nothing special‹. The restaurant soon closed again.

As we talk with Asaf, seated at a small table inside, food keeps appearing from the kitchen. We learn about what is grown and produced in Israel – and what is not; sometimes it is surprising. Tahini, for example, a classic ingredient of Israeli food, is not used in the kitchen at Dok because the sesame seeds nowadays generally come from Ethiopia.

In 2011, Asaf and Yotam opened Ha'Achim – The Brothers – right next door to Dok. It still remains the ›mothership‹ of the business, a larger restaurant serving Greek food. Ha'Achim at first seemed destined for failure as well, and Asaf and Yotam lost a great deal of money. However, thanks to professional support, the sale of alcohol at wholesale prices, and a DJ, Ha'Achim received its first favourable review in 2014 – finally success. At the same time the Carpaccio Bar closed down. The story really could have ended right there.

Yet, Asaf saw in the bar's space another chance to experiment. The idea of sustainability and a low carbon footprint had been on his mind, and he discussed it with his brother. He had always dreamed of placing plants and herbs at the forefront and demonstrating a strong connection with nature with the menu as well. He spent six months researching what products were available in the region; he visited producers all over Israel and found suppliers. His idea began to take shape. Dok opened in 2015, initially offering seven dishes that were all made completely with local ingredients. Today the restaurant offers up to twelve dishes, and the menu changes daily. Much is seasonal, such as wild capers or mulberries. Asaf is a purist. The culmination of his ideal of ›local‹ came when he found a small grove of trees bearing bitter oranges, merely a stone's throw from where we now sit in central Tel Aviv. He makes his own tonic with them.

Asaf speaks warmly of and with great respect for his suppliers, praising in particular the dairy farms that supply him with fresh products. He is willing to pay more for local cheeses than he would

for imported ones. He has many Arab suppliers who deliver oranges and vegetables from Jericho. The fact that wheat is not grown in Israel is not really a problem for the kitchen at Dok. But occasionally, when Asaf has a certain foreign ingredient in mind, he simply turns it into a local one: on one of his many trips he became enamoured of a Mexican plant called *papalo*, a herb that tastes similar to coriander (cilantro) and flourishes in warm regions. His stubbornness once again paid off: he found a farmer who now grows it for him here in Israel – which meant one more ›local‹ product for his kitchen.

For Asaf, Dok is a ›never-ending project‹ and its success is tied to him staying hands-on. However, as we drink one last glass of wine, he tells us that he likes to travel and has just returned from the Burning Man Festival in the U.S., where he cooked in the desert. Clearly, his determined focus on ›local‹ has not lessened his interest in the whole world.

STEWED CABBAGE WITH GOAT'S CHEESE & CHIMICHURRI

RECIPE FROM ASAF DOKTOR

For 4 people as a main dish

For the stewed cabbage:

- 1 large white cabbage, as young as possible (about 2 kg/4 lb 8 oz)
- 4 cherry tomatoes
- 1 acri sivri (cayenne) pepper
- 3 garlic cloves
- 175 ml (5¾ fl oz) white wine
- 10 sprigs za'atar or oregano
- 5 sprigs rosemary
- 5 sprigs sage
- 125 ml (4 fl oz) olive oil
- Sea salt

For the chimichurri:

- 30 g (1 oz) za'atar or oregano
- 1 spring onion (scallion)
- 2 garlic cloves
- Grated zest of 1 untreated lemon
- 1 teaspoon sea salt
- 1 teaspoon sugar
- 100 ml (3½ fl oz) red wine vinegar
- 160 ml (5¼ fl oz) olive oil

- 4 slices goat cheese roll (such as Sainte-Maure de Touraine)

For the *cabbage,* preheat the oven to 240°C (475°F). Line an ovenproof dish or a deep baking tray with aluminium foil and place the cabbage with the stem down on the foil (there should be enough foil to completely enclose the whole cabbage later).

Cut a hole 2–3 cm (about 1 inch) in diameter in the centre of the cabbage head, almost down to the root.

Quarter the cherry tomatoes and halve the sivri pepper. Peel the garlic and halve as well. Stuff the tomatoes, sivri pepper and garlic into the hole in the cabbage and pour in the white wine. Distribute the herbs evenly on and around the cabbage. Drizzle with olive oil, season inside and out with salt and wrap the aluminium foil firmly around the cabbage. Stew in the oven until the cabbage is very soft, about 2½ hours.

Meanwhile, prepare the *chimichurri*. Pluck the za'atar leaves from the stems and finely chop. Trim the spring onion, peel the garlic and finely chop both. Combine with the remaining ingredients in a bowl and marinate for 2 hours at room temperature.

Take the cabbage out of the oven and let cool for a bit. Then remove the foil and cut the cabbage into 8 wedges. Place on plates, spoon chimichurri over the top and sprinkle with a bit of salt. Arrange the goat's cheese on the cabbage and caramelise with a culinary torch. Serve warm.

FISH
FROM THE MEDITERRANEAN SEA
TO THE TABLE

FISH BURIKAS WITH SQUASH HARISSA

For 4 people as an appetiser

For the squash harissa:

- O 650 g (1 lb 7 oz) calabaza squash
- O 1 tablespoon sea salt
- O ½ teaspoon coriander seeds
- O ½ teaspoon cumin seeds
- O ½ teaspoon fennel seeds
- O ½ teaspoon caraway seeds
- O ½ teaspoon chilli flakes
- O 20 g (¾ oz) pickled lemons (page 97)
- O 1 garlic clove
- O 4½ teaspoons sugar
- O 6 tablespoons olive oil
- O 2 tablespoons harissa (page 95)

For the burikas:

- O 1 branzino fillet without skin (about 300 g/10½ oz)
- O 1 small spring onion (scallion)
- O 1 acri sivri (cayenne) pepper
- O ½ onion
- O 1 sprig dill
- O 3 sprigs coriander (cilantro)
- O 4 sprigs flat-leaf parsley
- O Grated zest of 1 untreated lime
- O 2 tablespoons dry breadcrumbs
- O 1 teaspoon sea salt
- O 2 tablespoons olive oil
- O Canola oil, for frying
- O 50 g (1¾ oz) plain flour
- O 4 spring roll wrappers
- O 4 egg yolks

Preheat oven to 220°C (425°F). For the *squash harissa*, peel and deseed the squash and cut into 3 cm (1¼ inch) cubes. Mix with the salt in an ovenproof dish, cover with aluminium foil and bake in the oven until the squash is soft and golden brown, 20–30 minutes. Remove from the oven and pour off the liquid.

Dry-roast the spices in a frying pan until they release their aromas, then finely grind them in a mortar. Blitz half of the squash together with the pickled lemon in a blender or with a stick blender to make a cream. Coarsely mash the remaining squash with a fork. Peel and finely chop the garlic, then mix together all the ingredients for the squash harissa. →

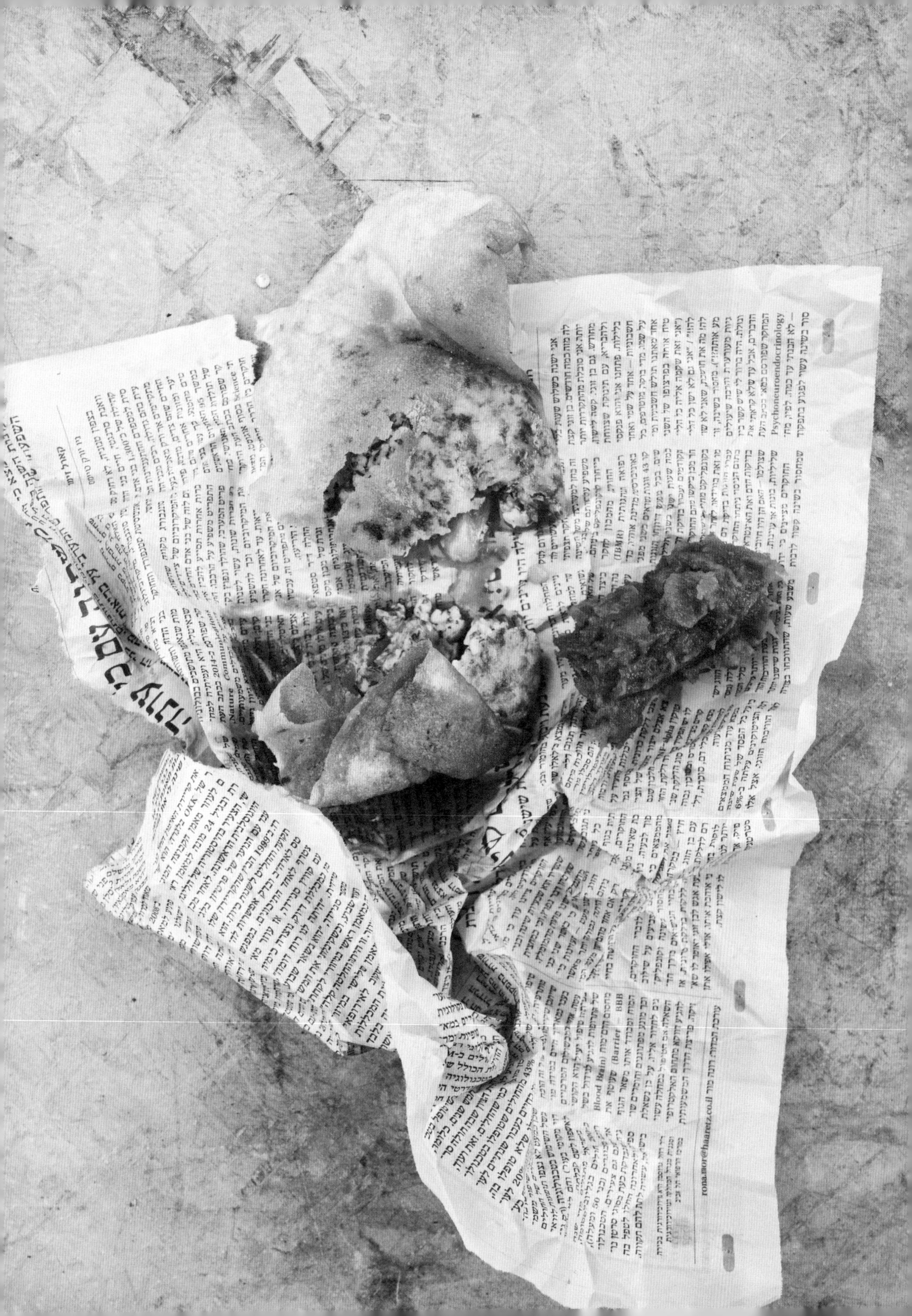
Psychoneuroendocrinology
rona.mor@haaretz.co.il

For the *burikas,* cut the branzino fillet into very fine dice. Trim the spring onion and finely chop. Deseed sivri pepper and finely dice. Peel onion and finely chop. Finely chop herbs with their stems. Combine the chopped ingredients with the lime zest, dry breadcrumbs, salt and olive oil and chop again until very fine or put through a meat grinder.

Heat an ample amount of canola oil in a deep saucepan. Whisk the flour together with 50 ml (1½ fl oz) of water until smooth. Lay out the spring roll wrappers flat. Place a quarter of the filling on each wrapper. In the middle of the filling, make a well and carefully place 1 egg yolk in it. Brush the edges of the wrappers with the flour-water mixture and fold into triangles. Press the sides firmly together so that no oil can penetrate during the frying process. Carefully flatten the filled wrappers a bit.

Fry the burikas in the hot oil until golden brown and crisp. Remove from the saucepan with a slotted spoon, drain on paper towels and serve with the squash harissa.

Elihay and his friends occasionally skipped school in Israel and spent their time in front of a tiny food truck parked on the street. There were only two items to choose from: falafel in pita bread, and burika with eggs. But the specialty of the rolling restaurant was a combination of the two: the crispy burika was stuffed into the soft pita, and with the first bite the crisp shell of the burika broke and the creamy filling spread over the whole bread. It was served with amba, tahini and chershi – a spicy pumpkin salad that the truck owner's grandmother, who originally came from Tripoli, Lebanon, made fresh every day. The NENI burikas with fish and fine herbs were inspired by this street food.

HAYA'S TIP:
LEFT-OVER SQUASH HARISSA WILL KEEP IN THE REFRIGERATOR FOR A WEEK AND IS DELICIOUS AS A SPREAD ON BREAD OR AN ACCOMPANIMENT TO EGGS AND FISH.

CHRAIME

For 4 people as a main dish

- O 600 g (1 lb 5 oz) fresh tomatoes (in winter, use grape tomatoes; in summer various kinds are suitable)
- O Sea salt
- O 3 red pointed peppers
- O 1 acri sivri (cayenne) pepper
- O 3 garlic cloves
- O 100 ml (3½ fl oz) olive oil, plus extra for drizzling
- O 400 g (14 oz) can peeled tomatoes
- O 800 g–1 kg (about 2 lb) branzino in one piece, or another kind of white filleted fish
- O 7 sprigs coriander (cilantro)

Cut out the stems of the fresh tomatoes and make a crisscross incision in the skin on the opposite end. Bring salted water (1 teaspoon salt per litre/35 fl oz water) to the boil in a saucepan, add the tomatoes and blanch for 1 minute. Immediately immerse the tomatoes in iced water, pull off the skin and quarter the skinned tomatoes.

Deseed the two kinds of peppers and dice. Peel and finely chop the garlic.

Put a large ovenproof saucepan over very high heat on the stove, briefly heat a small amount of olive oil in it, add the peppers and sauté briefly. Add the garlic and sauté along with the peppers for several seconds, then add the fresh and canned tomatoes and heat. Pour in the remaining olive oil and season with salt. Simmer, uncovered, for 20 minutes over medium heat. Season with salt to taste.

Preheat the oven grill to 260°C (500°F). Cut branzino into slices, season with salt lightly and add to the sauce. Cook under the hot grill for about 10 minutes.

Pluck the coriander leaves from the stems and coarsely chop. Remove the pan from the oven, drizzle the fish with olive oil and garnish with coriander. Serve hot.

HAYA'S TIPS:
GOOD ACCOMPANIMENTS TO THIS DISH ARE TAHINI (PAGE 94) AND SOURDOUGH BREAD, WHICH CAN BE DUNKED IN THE DELECTABLE SAUCE.

THE FISH CAN BE REPLACED WITH PRAWNS (JUMBO SHRIMP), CALAMARI OR OCTOPUS.
WHEN TOMATOES ARE IN SEASON, I FREQUENTLY COOK A LARGER BATCH OF SAUCE AND FREEZE IT.

HAYA'S TIP:
THE PASTE WILL KEEP AT LEAST
10 DAYS IN THE REFRIGERATOR.

IKRA BRUSCHETTA

For 4–6 people as an appetiser

- O 15 g (½ oz) white bread, crust removed (such as challa, page 253)
- O 25 ml (¾ fl oz) milk
- O 50 g (1¾ oz) carp roe
- O 1 onion
- O ½ teaspoon sea salt
- O 350 ml (12 fl oz) grape seed oil, or canola oil
- O 2 tablespoons sparking mineral water
- O Juice of ½ lemon
- O 4–6 slices sourdough bread
- O 1 red onion
- O 1 handful kalamata olives
- O Olive oil, for drizzling

In keeping with Jewish tradition, no cooking was done on Shabbat in Haya's family. Her mother even gave up her beloved cigarettes on this day.

In Tel Aviv, the large Romanian family went out to eat every Saturday to Haim Nello, a legendary restaurant that still exists. They served the best ikra in the city there, garnished with finely sliced onions and black olives and served with brown bread. When the family moved to Bremen, a new tradition was started: they no longer went to Nello but always to a ›Wienerwald‹ chain restaurant, and instead of ikra the family ate grilled chicken and goulash soup.

Soak bread in milk; then press out all liquid. Remove roe from the sac and wash thoroughly. Peel onion, finely grate, wrap in a tea towel and press out the liquid.

Beat bread, roe, 2 tablespoons of the grated onion and the salt in a blender or with a stick blender until light and fluffy. While the blender is running, slowly pour in the oil in a thin stream, also gradually adding the mineral water and lemon juice in turn. This gives the paste a mayonnaise-like consistency.

Toast the sourdough bread. Peel the red onion and cut into thin rings. Pit the olives and either chop or leave whole.

Spread the bread slices with the paste and garnish with olives. To finish, drizzle with olive oil.

OCTOPUS ON A SKEWER

For 4 people as an appetiser

For the octopus:

- O 1 kg (2 lb 4 oz) octopus (have your fish seller clean it for you)
- O 1 small onion
- O 1 acri sivri (cayenne) pepper
- O 3–4 sprigs flat-leaf parsley
- O 2 bay leaves
- O 3 tablespoons olive oil
- O Sea salt

For the marinade:

- O 4½ teaspoons maple syrup
- O 2 teaspoons white miso paste
- O 25 g (1 oz) harissa (page 95)
- O 25 g (1 oz) pickled lemons (page 97)
- O 3 tablespoons olive oil

HAYA'S TIPS: THE MARINATED OCTOPUS CAN ALSO BE COOKED ON AN OUTSIDE GRILL, OF COURSE. WHEN WE DO THIS IN ISRAEL, WE OFTEN USE A SHARPENED OLIVE BRANCH AS A SKEWER.

ASK YOUR FISH SELLER TO GUT THE OCTOPUS AND CUT OFF THE MIDDLE PART OF THE HEAD WITH THE EYES. THE REST OF THE HEAD CAN BE COOKED WITH THE BODY.

Wash the *octopus* under running water so that the suckers are clean. Halve the onion (leaving the skin on) and sivri pepper. Put octopus, onion, sivri, parsley, bay leaves and 1 tablespoon olive oil in a large saucepan. Add enough water to completely cover the octopus. Toss in 1 tablespoon salt per litre (35 fl oz) of water.

Bring water to the boil, reduce to medium heat and cook the octopus until soft (a bit like a cooked chicken breast), about 45–60 minutes. Remove from the heat and let the octopus cool in the cooking water for about 1 hour.

For the *marinade,* blitz all ingredients until smooth in a blender or with a stick blender.

Remove octopus from the water and carefully pull off any skin that has come loose during cooking. Separate the tentacles from the body, mix with 2 tablespoons olive oil and lightly season with salt. Thread each tentacle onto a metal skewer.

Place a chargrill pan over high heat and sear the octopus tentacles until they are crisp and golden brown. Then brush with the marinade and grill again briefly. Serve directly from the pan.

Offering a person something to eat is a wonderful and respectful gesture. It invites the person to come closer, and a personal connection is immediately established. Sharing with others also testifies to the special value of a homemade meal. The inspiration for this dish was, once again, Israeli street food. At your next barbecue, hand each of your guests a skewer directly from the fire – a gesture that connects.

THE ARTISTS

YAEL & KEREN STELLEGOFEN

Habanot Ohevot Ochel
»The Artists«

»We're very different in our loves and likes.«

›Women love food.‹ That is both the name of their business, Habanot Ohevot Ochel, and the inspiration for the teamwork of Yael and Keren Stellegofen, both as a couple and professionally. Between them, they assume many roles: artist, dancer, cook, baker, businesswoman, and most recently, parent. Together, they cook, bake and host collective dinners that can be booked online; the guests, who have never met, then come together to spend an evening enjoying good food and conversation.

We enter an old building with a large adjacent rooftop terrace and climb a narrow staircase with graffiti-covered walls to meet the two women behind Habanot. Nothing prepares you for the drama of the space with its old walls of beautifully textured peeling paint in faded blues, its high ceilings, and art displayed everywhere. This large loft, once an artist's studio, is now the venue for the Stellegofens' communal dinners. In a room next to the terrace there is still a studio space filled with paints, canvases and sculptures; this is where Keren paints and draws whenever she finds the time. The main room is dominated by a long, massive table, and modern lamps offset the old walls. The centre of activity is the kitchen, just off the dining room.

We hear the cries of a baby coming from the nearby bedroom. Yael just recently gave birth to a little girl. Yael and Keren, as proud first-time parents, take us to meet their baby, who is being well cared for during our conversation by safta (grandma). We return to the table to find out more about our hosts. Both Yael and Keren were born in Tel Aviv. Yael grew up in Jerusalem; she seems to be the quieter of the two, while Keren is clearly more gregarious.

Yael, whose grandmother had Persian and German roots, recalls that when she was a child there was rarely ›real‹ food in the house, mostly just chocolate and chocolate pudding – rather unusual for someone who makes her living in the food business! Her first passion, however, was dance: she began dancing at the age of seven and eventually had a successful career with the Barak Marshall Dance Theatre in Tel Aviv. Only after finishing her university degree in art and theatre did she trade the world of dance for that of the food business. Yael quickly realised that she preferred this kind of hands-on experience and first specialised in pastry making. She developed a particular interest in making bread while working at the well-known Lachmanina bakery.

Keren's food beginnings were quite different. Her father is Israeli and her mother comes from the U.S. Her mother is a great cook, and Keren grew up eating simple but healthy American food. There was meat, chicken and oven-baked turkey, lots of fresh vegetables and not much fried food. When Keren made her first trip to London as a child, she ordered steak and artichokes! Keren studied photography and art intermittently for ten years and earned two degrees. She found her way into the kitchen after only one day of waitressing at the well-known fish restaurant Farida in Herzliya. Soon she was responsible for the large oven containing eighteen shelves for cooking fish – and she loved the challenge. Although at that time she did not even know ›how to hold a knife‹, as she recalls, she realised that professional cooking was what she wanted to do. After a period of travel, Keren spent four years working at the now-famous CoffeeBar (page 171).

Yael and Keren met in 2012 on a blind date and married the following year, although their marriage is still not officially recognised in Israel. They honeymooned in Italy and upon their return to Tel Aviv lived first in a loft in the Florentin neighbourhood and then eventually moved to Neve Tzedek. Keren dedicated herself to art, while Yael worked as a cook and manager at restaurants and also began baking and making jams at home to sell.

The catering business began a year and a half later. They did not want to open a conventional restaurant, especially since Keren was still devoting herself completely to her art work. At first they catered small events and put up a menu on Facebook for take-away food. Eventually they began offering cooking classes at home, reaching interested people through EatWith, an online platform that brings people together through communal cooking. They worked long hours but could always count on the support of their families. This was the birth of Habanot Ohevot Ochel.

Soon they had more guests than their small apartment in the now-trendy area of Neve Tzedek could accommodate. They recognised that they needed a bigger place for their dinners. So three years ago they moved here, near Rothschild Boulevard in the centre of Tel Aviv. The place was in very poor condition, and Yael and Keren had only one week to renovate it. Partitions were removed, the kitchen was refurnished, and they were able to receive their first guests in an apartment with a raw, urban character. They now host dinners four evenings a week at which strangers mingle, as well as doing occasional rooftop parties with a DJ. Business is booming.

When it comes to cooking, Keren prefers simple food, and she especially loves seafood. Her culinary style is Mediterranean, using simple ingredients such as olive oil, lemon, oregano and za'atar. Everything is fresh and seasonal. Yael does all the baking, and they are constantly thinking about how best to align the cooked foods and the baked goods. Their dinners consist of six to seven courses, with wine flowing freely. They offer a wide range of food: for example, one winter menu centres on whisky and pork, while another offers an interpretation of choucroute garnie. We visited them in late summer, and sampled the wonderful fresh seafood and knafeh. Dessert is always a pleasantly light conclusion to Keren's meals.

When we meet, they are preparing for their first dinner following a brief break for the birth of their daughter. Yael and Keren still need to find out together how to reconcile baby with business and what changes might need to be made in their working lives. They hope that Keren can also one day bear a child. Different as they are, these two talented artists, these ›women who love food‹, complement each other brilliantly: together they have produced a creative and thriving place where people gather around the long table for delicious communal dinners.

ISRAELI SEAFOOD PAELLA

RECIPE FROM YAEL AND KEREN STELLEGOFEN

For 6–8 people as a main dish

For the croutons:

- O 3 slices sourdough bread, flatbread or challa (1 day old)
- O 1 tablespoon dried za'atar spice mix
- O 2 tablespoons olive oil

For the marinated za'atar:

- O 1 small red onion
- O 2 bunches fresh za'atar or oregano
- O 2 tablespoons sumac
- O Juice of ½ lemon
- O 2 tablespoons olive oil
- O ½ teaspoon sea salt

For the stewed tomatoes:

- O 2.5 kg (5 lb 8 oz) multicoloured cherry tomatoes
- O 4 garlic cloves
- O 3 tablespoons olive oil
- O 1 tablespoon sea salt
- O 1 teaspoon black pepper

- O 20 calamari
- O 12 prawns (jumbo shrimp)
- O Olive oil
- O 100 g (3½ oz) feta cheese
- O 1 lime
- O Fresh za'atar, to garnish
- O Sumac, for sprinkling

Preheat oven to 200°C (400°F). For the *croutons,* tear bread into coarse pieces and combine with the dried za'atar spice mix and the olive oil on a baking tray lined with baking paper.

Roast in the oven until the bread is golden brown and crispy, about 15 minutes. Remove from the oven and set aside.

While the bread roasts, marinate the *za'atar*. Peel the onion and cut into thin slices. Pluck the za'atar leaves from the stems. Mix both together in a bowl with the sumac, lemon juice, olive oil and salt and let rest for at least 10 minutes.

For the *stewed tomatoes,* heat the oven grill to 260°C (500°F). Quarter the tomatoes and peel the garlic. Mix all ingredients together on a baking tray lined with baking paper and cook under the hot grill for 20 minutes, so that the tomatoes give off a bit of liquid. Take out and set aside.

Clean the calamari and prawns. Heat a chargrill pan and brush with a bit of olive oil. Cook the seafood, turning after 1–2 minutes. Grill the other side for 1–2 minutes and lift out of the pan. (The prawns are done as soon as they turn pink. The calamari should be lightly browned.)

Coarsely crumble the feta and quarter the lime. Arrange the seafood and croutons on plates with the stewed tomatoes. Add the feta and lime quarters and garnish with the marinated and the fresh za'atar and with the sumac.

SAVOURY KNAFEH WITH FRIED CHERRY TOMATOES

RECIPE FROM YAEL AND KEREN STELLEGOFEN

For 4 people as a main dish

- O 250 g (9 oz) mascarpone cheese
- O 200 g (7 oz) soft goat's cheese
- O 1 tablespoon dried za'atar spice mix
- O 250 ml (9 fl oz) cream
- O Sea salt
- O 100 g (3½ oz) butter, melted
- O 300 g (10½ oz) kataifi pastry (angel hair)
- O Olive oil
- O 1 handful cherry tomatoes
- O Yoghurt, for drizzling
- O Za'atar leaves or oregano, to garnish

Preheat oven to 220°C (425°F). Blitz the mascarpone, soft goat's cheese and za'atar in a blender. Add the cream and blitz for 2 more minutes at moderate speed. Season to taste with salt.

Melt butter in a small saucepan. On a work surface or in a bowl, pull apart the kataifi pastry strings a bit with your hands, pour the butter over the top and knead together well. (This makes the dough strings more elastic and easier to work with.) Place half of the dough strings in a 28 cm (11 inch) round cake tin lined with baking paper. Spread the cheese mixture over the top and cover with the second half of the dough. Bake until golden brown, about 15 minutes.

While the knafeh cooks, heat a chargrill pan until very hot. Pour in a bit of olive oil, add the cherry tomatoes and cook for a few seconds; until lightly browned but still intact. Season with salt.

Remove the knafeh from the oven, cut into 4 pieces and arrange on plates. Drizzle with yoghurt, garnish with cherry tomatoes and za'atar leaves and serve immediately.

DEEP-FRIED SARDINES WITH GREEN AIOLI

For 4 people as an appetiser

For the green aioli:
- O 270 ml (9 fl oz) grape seed oil
- O 125 ml (4 fl oz) olive oil
- O 2 garlic cloves
- O 1 acri sivri (cayenne) pepper
- O 1 whole egg
- O 1 egg yolk
- O ½ teaspoon sea salt
- O 1 sprig flat-leaf parsley
- O 1 teaspoon lime juice
- O 1 teaspoon red wine vinegar

For the sardines:
- O Canola oil, for deep-frying
- O Sea salt
- O Wheat or chickpea flour, for dusting
- O 250 g (9 oz) sardines (have your fish seller clean them for you)
- O Chimichurri sauce (page 119), to serve

For the *aioli*, mix both oils together. Peel the garlic and deseed sivri pepper. Purée both, along with all the remaining ingredients except the oil, until smooth with a stick blender or in a blender. Slowly pour in the oil in a thin stream while blending, until you have a creamy, homogeneous mixture.

For the *sardines,* heat the canola oil in a deep saucepan. Mix salt and flour and spread on a plate. Toss the sardines in the flour and deep-fry them in the hot oil until golden brown. Remove with a slotted spoon and drain on paper towels.

Serve the crispy sardines with the aioli and the chimichurri sauce.

HAYA'S TIPS:

SINCE IT IS DIFFICULT TO MAKE A SMALL AMOUNT OF AIOLI, I ALWAYS MAKE A BIT MORE OF IT – AS I DO HERE. IT KEEPS IN THE REFRIGERATOR FOR 5–6 DAYS.

IN ISRAEL, PEOPLE OFTEN EAT THE SMALL, DEEP-FRIED SARDINES ON THE STREET WITH THEIR HANDS, LIKE FRENCH FRIES. SARDINES ARE ESPECIALLY ATTRACTIVE WHEN SERVED IN A PAPER CONE.

CALAMARI WITH ROASTED CHERRY TOMATOES

For 2–3 people as an appetiser

- 200 g (7 oz) calamari, with the heads (small to medium calamari)
- Sea salt
- 6 tablespoons olive oil
- 200 g (7 oz) cherry tomatoes
- 1 acri sivri (cayenne) pepper
- 4 spring onions (scallions)
- 30 g (1 oz) pickled lemons (page 97)
- 1 garlic clove
- 10 mint leaves
- 20 coriander (cilantro) leaves
- 50 g (1¾ oz) Greek yoghurt

Clean the calamari and cut open each of the tubes on one side from the opening to the tip. Place flat on a chopping board with the inner surface facing up. With a knife, score the flesh first lengthways and then widthwise without cutting all the way through, resulting in a grid-like pattern. Place the tubes in a bowl with the heads, season with salt and mix with 5 tablespoons olive oil. Allow calamari to marinate until you are ready to use them.

Preheat oven to 240°C (475°F). Lay the cherry tomatoes on a baking tray or in an ovenproof dish, drizzle with 1 tablespoon olive oil and roast in the oven for 15 minutes.

Meanwhile, deseed the sivri pepper and slice into thin rings. Clean the spring onions, slice the white parts diagonally into thin rings and cut the green parts into 3–4 cm (1½ inch) pieces. Finely chop the pickled lemon; peel the garlic and cut into thin slices.

Heat a very large, heavy-based saucepan over very high heat until it starts to smoke – take care because it is then extremely hot! Lay the calamari tubes flat next to each other on the bottom of the pan with the scored sides down; they should not touch each other or overlap. Then add the heads. Sear until the calamari are golden brown, about 2 minutes. (The tubes will roll up when seared.) Remove and set aside.

Add the white parts of the spring onions to the pan and roast them. Add the cherry tomatoes and sivri and roast for another 30 seconds. Then add, one after another, the garlic, lemon, spring onion greens and herbs, briefly tossing together after each addition. Finally, pour 2 tablespoons water into the pan and scrape up the drippings from the bottom. (This helps the flavours mingle with the ingredients, and the water will evaporate through the heat.)

Arrange calamari and tomatoes on plates and serve with Greek yoghurt.

HAYA'S TIPS:
THIS DISH IS VERY EASILY PREPARED, BUT THE DETAILS ARE IMPORTANT. FIRST: THE PAN MUST BE SUFFICIENTLY HOT, WHICH MEANS HEATING IT FOR AT LEAST 4–5 MINUTES OVER THE HIGHEST HEAT.

SECOND: THE CALAMARI NEED SUFFICIENT SPACE IN THE PAN; IT IS BETTER TO COOK THEM IN TWO STAGES THAN TO FRY TOO MUCH AT ONCE. THIRD: DON'T COOK THE CALAMARI FOR TOO LONG OR THEY WILL BECOME RUBBERY.

THE FISHERMAN AND THE WRITER

SAADO ZEINAB & GILI SASSOWER

»The Fisherman and the Writer«

This will be a story of great loyalties and great hardships. For millennia, boats have found refuge in the Jaffa port and fishermen have set out from here to cast their nets and sink their lines. Gili Sassower picks us up at one of the port's tourist cafes; without him we would not be admitted to the nearby boatyard to meet Gili's colleague and friend Saado Zeinab, Head of the Jaffa Fishermen's Union. On the way there we meet Mahmoud, known as Moumou, Saado's nephew. Gili calls him ›the best fisherman in Jaffa‹. He is a wiry young man with a deep scar on his forehead. He fishes from midnight until 6 a.m., hauling in the best fish in town.

We head to an almost finished fishing trawler, dry-docked right next to the high seawall, the peeling and salt-encrusted barrier to the Mediterranean. The sea is calm this morning. Saado and Gili have been working on this trawler for several years. Gili smiles as he tells us that only the fibreglass finish remains to be done, but this is Saado's boat and he seems in no hurry to make it seaworthy; it has become a sort of home base for him at the Jaffa port. As we climb a steep flight of steps, we are welcomed up onto the roomy deck by Saado, his strong features radiating a warm-hearted countenance. He invites us to sit under a sun canopy of old sails strung together, and we settle onto comfortable cushions next to a wooden table where we are served coffee with cardamom. We immediately sense the deep bond between Saado, the eighth-generation Arab fisherman, and Gili, his younger Jewish companion. They are bound closely together by mutual affection and loyalty and by their common struggle with an imperilled sea and the hard way of life it offers.

We look out at this ancient sea, which is threatened in many ways. It is becoming warmer, more saline, and an increasing number of oil and natural gas platforms close to shore could do immense damage with one spill. Fishermen are crucially dependent on space in the Jaffa port itself. They have led the fight against government efforts to privatise the port in the early '90s, and they currently struggle to preserve the use of hangars, lobbying to keep workspaces from being gentrified for tourism. Fishery is only a small sector of the Israeli economy. Israel consumes 80,000 tons of fish per annum, of which local fishermen provide only 2,700 tons. The rest is imported, usually frozen, in containers from countries such as China, which count their tonnages in the millions. The government here has other priorities. Saado, head of the local Fishermen's Union, has been jailed in the past for leading demonstrations, voicing his concern directly to the government in Jerusalem. Gili shares some of the risks and supports the union struggle as Saado's secretary.

Saado is the oldest active fisherman here and patriarch of Jaffa's largest family of fishermen, which operates a total of 25 boats. Saado has five sons and two daughters, and this port is their territory. Several years ago, one of Saado's sons was stopped by the military police and asked for his ID. The son replied that a policeman of the first generation here has no right to interrogate someone of the ninth generation.

Gili comes from a very different world. He was born in Haifa into a wealthy family with German and Eastern European roots. Many of his relatives were involved in the shipping industry. Gili served in the navy and has always felt connected to the sea and to fishermen. In 2003 he moved to Jaffa, where he was surrounded by artists and bohemian types. He lived next door to Saado and his family. One day, Gili received an invitation from Saado: ›Come and fish with us, and we'll make a man out of you.‹

Things were different back when Saado's grandfather was fishing. There were more fish and fewer fishermen. Asked about the future, Saado says with

a smile that until now the farthest any family member has ventured away from fishing was to open a fish store in Jaffa. He does not know what life his grandchildren will have; he only knows that it is important that they go to school and receive a good education.

Gili is fiercely protective of this way of life. Since his fishing date with Saado's family, Gili has not only worked on a lot of boats with many different people, he has also published two novels and a seminal book about the sea: *Mare Nostrum – Marinot* gives the fishermen of Jaffa a name as well as a face in wonderful black-and-white portraits. The book lists 81 species of fish, gives their names in Hebrew, Arabic and English, provides information about each species and its habitat through the seasons, and describes the role fish play in folklore. It also contains instructions for processing fish and a number of recipes. The book is now out of print but remains an important reference work for the chefs of Tel Aviv. Gili is already at work on a new project: a book based on his fishing column, 52 Days, published in the newspaper *Haaretz*. He laughingly says: ›Marine biologists know a lot about the sea but not much about fishing.‹

Saado brings us more coffee. Here on his boat he welcomes people regardless of where they come from. ›We have a lot of respect for everyone,‹ he says. A life full of hardship is written into Saado's face, but at the same time he radiates warmth. He is proud to be a fisherman, and thus independent. He started fishing at age four; he never attended school but was taught by his grandfather. Today he is an accomplished designer of boats and an expert on diesel motors, keeping everything in his head without making blueprints or sketches. He has built most of his boats himself. This boat seems to be a peaceful haven in difficult times.

Gili reminds us that there is an ongoing struggle for use of the sea. Gas from the sea is a current threat for the fishermen, and prior to every election, promises are made by politicians, which are often not kept. Resistance is fragmented; some issues divide the fishermen amongst themselves. The Union does not have an effective national representation, so each port is on its own. Bureaucratic obstacles, a lack of support from authorities and racism against Arabs make the work of the fishermen here more difficult. The ongoing Israeli-Palestinian conflict also leaves scars. Saado remembers the close ties he had to fishing families in the Gaza Strip – many of whom are relatives – and the visits and mutual support. Now the telephone is the only contact, as personal visits are not possible. Saado says wistfully: ›It was good being together.‹ Gili has also often experienced violence here and has been personally threatened because of his role in the union and his close relationship to Saado's family. He is not certain he will spend his entire life here at the port, although he and Saado cannot imagine that they would ever go their separate ways.

Despite these hardships, Saado still maintains an optimistic outlook. It's September when we visit the two men; the water is slowly growing cooler in the port, which was once called the ›gate to the temple of Solomon‹. By November, explains Saado, the fish will move closer to the shore and many more boats will be out. We feel at ease on Saado's boat. Perhaps it will also set out to catch shark and other large fish. We ask Saado when his trawler will be finished. He smiles, points to another nearby boat, and says: ›That one will definitely be finished in three months.‹

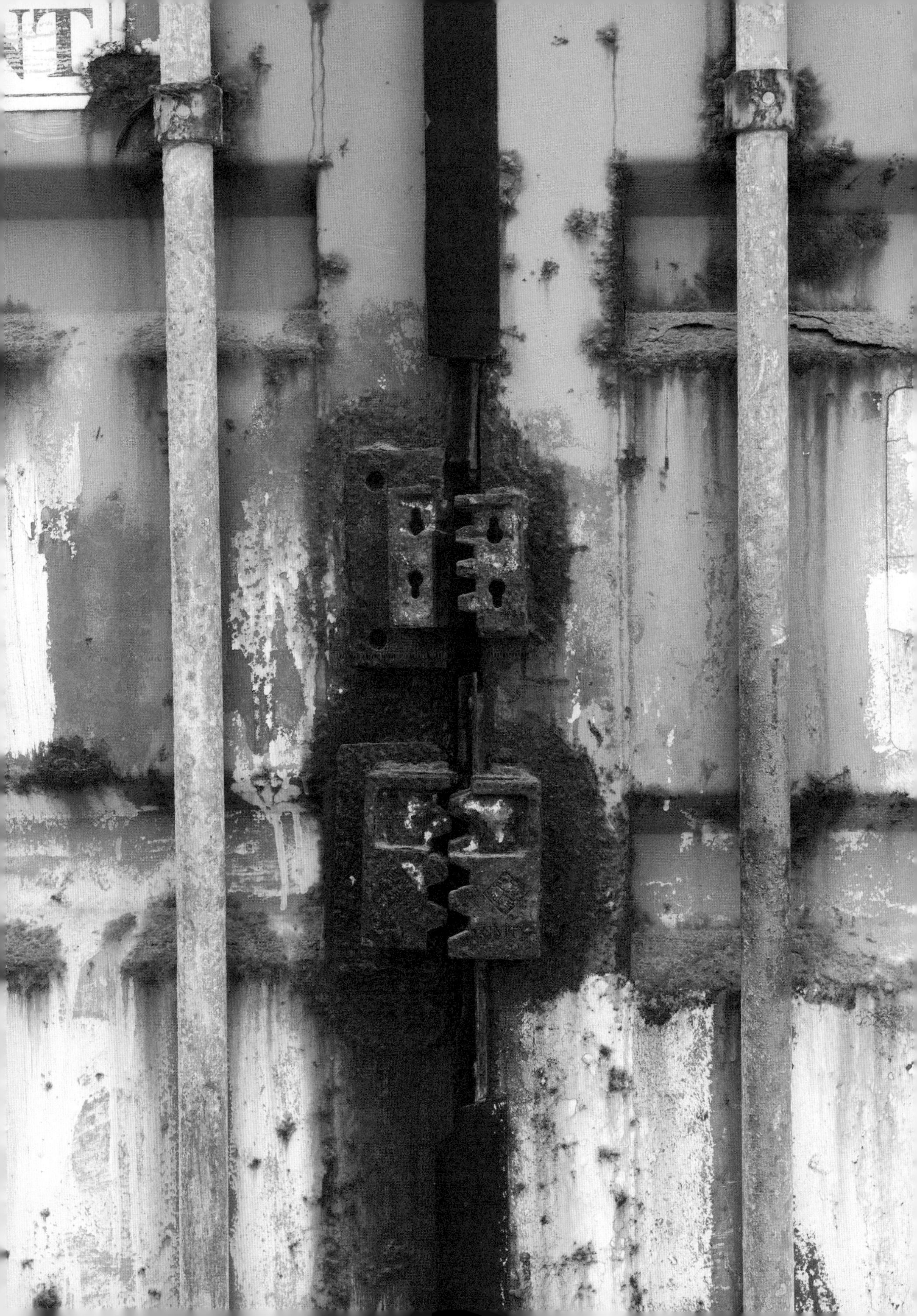

»We have a lot of respect for everyone.«

המקום של בון בון
חטיפים
Big
$ ATM €
LIQUOR STORE
CHOCOLATE SHOP
CALLING CARDS
STAMPS
MOBILE ACCESSORIES
COFFE TO GO
המקום של בון בון

FOCACCIA WITH BEETROOT & MARINATED SALMON

For 4 people as a main dish

For the marinated salmon:
- O 300 g (10½ oz) sugar
- O 300 g (10½ oz) sea salt
- O 1 tablespoon coriander seeds
- O 1 handful dill sprigs
- O 1 kg (2 lb 4 oz) salmon fillet, with skin

For the beetroot:
- O 2–3 beetroot
- O 100 ml (3½ fl oz) cider vinegar
- O 50 g (1¾ oz) sugar
- O 30 g (1 oz) salt
- O Crushed white pepper

For the pickled onions:
- O 125 g (4½ oz) red onions
- O 5 black peppercorns
- O 1 small bay leaf
- O 1 sprig thyme
- O 50 ml (1½ fl oz) water
- O 100 ml (3½ fl oz) rice vinegar
- O ½ teaspoon sea salt
- O 1 teaspoon sugar

- O 4 small balls of risen focaccia dough (page 93)
- O Flour, for working the dough
- O 4 tablespoons olive oil
- O 200 g (7 oz) crème fraîche

For the *marinated salmon,* mix together sugar and salt. Crush coriander seeds in a mortar and finely chop the dill (including the stems). Lay the salmon, skin side down, on a large high-rimmed plate or in an ovenproof dish and sprinkle the fleshy side with the coriander and dill, gently pressing in the herbs with your fingertips. Cover with the sugar-salt mixture and let rest for 12 hours in the refrigerator.

Remove the salmon from the fridge and wash under running water so the salt and sugar are rinsed off but a bit of dill still sticks to the fish. Drain on paper towels and blot dry. Then cover the salmon and leave it to rest for another 12 hours in the refrigerator. During this time the salt mixture, which has already permeated the outer layer, will seep into the inside of the fish. Finally, cut into thin slices at a slight angle to the skin.

Put the *beetroot,* cider vinegar, sugar, salt and pepper in a saucepan and cover with water. Simmer until the beetroot is soft, about 2–2½ hours, then immediately immerse in cold water and peel. Cut the beetroot into thin slices with a knife or a mandoline slicer.

Preheat oven to 110°C (225°F). Peel and halve *onions* and cut into very thin slices. Layer the onions, peppercorns, bay leaf and thyme alternately in a glass jar. →

Bring water, rice vinegar, salt and sugar to the boil and pour over the onions to completely fill the jar. Carefully seal jar. Fill an ovenproof dish or a deep roasting tin half-full with tepid water. Place the jar in the water and steam in the oven for 45 minutes. This can also be done in a steam cooker.

Preheat oven to it highest temperature, ideally 290°C (550°F), heating a pizza stone or inverted metal baking tray in the oven as well.

Roll the focaccia dough balls in flour and, working with your fingertips on a floured surface, carefully push the dough outwards from the centre (don't pull), shaping each ball into a flatbread with a 1 cm (½ inch) high edge. Lift the dough from the work surface and carefully stretch it outwards all the way around until it has a diameter of 25 cm (10 inches), keeping the edge of the dough in the flat of your hand.

Pull the dough onto a lightly floured wooden paddle, pierce the centre several times with a fork and slide onto the pizza stone or the back of the baking tray. Bake in the oven until golden brown, 3–5 minutes.

Remove the crispy flatbread from the oven. Layer with slices of beetroot and season with salt. Top with the salmon and pickled onions. Drizzle with olive oil and garnish with crème fraîche.

HAYA'S TIPS:
FOR THIS DISH, ONE REQUIRES A PROPER TIMETABLE. THE SALMON NEEDS TO MARINATE FOR 24 HOURS, AND THE FOCACCIA DOUGH SHOULD BE MADE AND LEFT TO RISE AT LEAST 12 HOURS BEFORE BAKING. IF YOU USE A PRESSURE COOKER, THE COOKING TIME FOR THE BEETROOT IS REDUCED TO 1 HOUR.

THE PICKLED ONIONS KEEP FOR SEVERAL MONTHS, SO YOU CAN MAKE A LARGER AMOUNT TO HAVE ON HAND. INSTEAD OF PICKLED ONIONS, YOU CAN ALSO USE FRESH RED ONIONS, BRIEFLY SOAKED IN VINEGAR AND WATER.

SINCE MOST OVENS ARE NOT LARGE ENOUGH TO BAKE FOUR FLATBREADS AT ONCE, SIMPLY PUT THE TOPPINGS ON THE FIRST FINISHED FLATBREAD, CUT INTO QUARTERS AND ENJOY IT TOGETHER WHILE THE NEXT ONE BAKES IN THE OVEN.

THE EPICURES

MAOZ ALONIM & ITAI HARGIL

HaBasta

»The Epicures«

What do two resourceful friends do when they find a spot for their new restaurant, intend to open two days later but are reminded by their accountant that their ›baby‹ still doesn't have a name? Maoz and Itai simply took a look over at the stands of the Carmel Market and they had it: *basta* means stall in Hebrew, so HaBasta was the logical choice. This all happened ten years ago, and HaBasta has now become a hotspot for people who love good food. Haya, who likes stopping by here for brunch on the weekend, describes the atmosphere affectionately as ›fine dining with flea-market charm‹.

HaBasta is located on a side street only a few steps from the Carmel Market, but it is as if one were entering a new world. Nuriel describes this neighbourhood: ›The market is like a busy highway: full, loud and hectic. But when you turn off it and walk into HaBasta, it is suddenly quiet; it is an oasis, and you feel like you are on vacation.‹ It is where his father, Samy, also grew up and where the whole family still feels at home.

As spontaneous as this name-giving may have been for the HaBasta owners, the idea of opening a restaurant near the busy market had been on their minds for a while. Maoz, who had arrived in Tel Aviv ten years earlier, had already established good connections with the merchants at the Carmel Market. He dreamed of a restaurant for which fresh ingredients would be purchased every morning at the market and where the menu would be determined by what was bought that day. And that is just how it is: HaBasta's menu is never written before 11 a.m. We arrive at the restaurant when the kitchen staff has just finished deciding on the food they will make that day. On the outside patio with French cafe-style chairs and 1950s tables, things are already getting busy. We find a quiet corner with Itai and Maoz, and new delicacies are constantly brought to our table from the kitchen. We are also served wine while we talk.

Itai and Maoz are bonded through a close friendship and a great passion for the restaurant business. They laugh a lot: two epicures who enjoy food and drink together at midday. Before opening HaBasta, they had both cooked at the Yoezer Wine Bar, whose owner was the late Shaul Evron, an influential restaurateur and pioneering food writer.

Maoz grew up in Haifa in a family of vegetarians where wine was served at every meal. He spent some of his childhood years in Zurich and did not serve in the army or attend university, which is highly unusual in Israel. At age 14, Maoz knew what his occupation would be: he left school and started working in restaurants and wine bars, opening his own bar in Haifa when he was still quite young.

Itai's parents both liked to cook; he calls his mother, who was born in Poland, ›an incredible cook‹. His parents kept kosher but the children did occasionally get to eat pork. Itai learned to cook at an early age by simply going into the kitchen and experimenting. His Ashkenazi/Polish/Russian roots are reflected in his cooking, but so are his travels through Israel, Europe and India. Itai and Maoz talk with us animatedly about food and drink, but also about their families and life in Israel. Occasionally they wave towards the kitchen to make sure that more food is on the way. Like many people here, they find the question of what defines Israeli food difficult to answer. Local food had existed for ages and then, after the founding of Israel, the different culinary styles blended together. For Itai, food in Tel Aviv – and in their restaurant – is the sum of

»Israelis are much closer to Egyptians than to the Swiss.«

all parts. He talks happily about what is being prepared in HaBasta's kitchen right now: beef tartar, okra, shawarma, pork belly, as well as oysters and raw fish. Maoz proudly tells us that they are one of only about ten restaurants in Tel Aviv that get fresh fish from the region. Gili, the fish merchant from our interview at the port of Jaffa (see page 148), supplies them with fish and Saado's best crabs. At HaBasta, the fish that is not freshly processed is cured in salt so that nothing goes to waste. Salted fish, Itai tells us, comes from the Ashkenazi culinary tradition and is delicious.

The choice of wines at HaBasta is truly impressive: its wine list is highly sophisticated and one of the largest in Israel, with a focus on selections from Burgundy and Piedmont. More wine is poured as the conversation turns to wine and politics. Maoz and Itai tell us that wine culture in Israel is growing stronger but many of the vineyards are in the Israeli-occupied territories. Because of their political convictions, Maoz and Itai do not work with wine growers who are Israeli settlers in the occupied territories. Itai has close links to Palestinian chefs in Nazareth and other places in the occupied territory. HaBasta regularly hosts a Palestinian evening in which the regular menu is influenced by this cultural focus.

The wine list at HaBasta lists the wines from Palestine separately from those from Israel, a controversial practice. However, Maoz does this intentionally in order to make a clear statement. For him as well as for Itai, HaBasta is a manifestation of their political views.

Despite all the political difficulties, Maoz sees Tel Aviv as a big, open city displaying many European influences but still closely linked with the rest of the Middle East. Having spent some of his early years in Zurich, Maoz sees it this way: ›In terms of their mentality,‹ he says, ›Israelis are much closer to Egyptians than to the Swiss.‹

Maoz and Itai recently handed over the responsibility for the restaurant's day-to-day business operations: Itai to Elon, who is now head chef; and Maoz to Aviram, who now acts as sommelier and general manager as well. In Tel Aviv, everybody knows everybody else – and this is especially true of HaBasta.

Despite all of these recent developments, HaBasta remains a source of energy for the two owners. Both Maoz and Itai are frequently present here, but now they have more time for their families. Both have small children, cook at home and have wives who are not involved in the restaurant business. Maoz is flying to Cambridge the day after we talk to take up residence there for a time while his partner completes her PhD there in international law and human rights.

There are no present plans for expanding HaBasta. They might add a regular daily breakfast to the menu. The discussion that breaks out over this is just as good-natured and uncomplicated as everything else that our cheerful and laid-back hosts discuss with each other. Maoz and Itai are satisfied with their life: ›It is good the way it is.‹ We couldn't have said it better ourselves.

CRAB BUREKAS

RECIPE FROM MAOZ ALONIM AND ITAI HARGIL

For 4 people as an appetiser

- O 1 potato
- O Sea salt
- O ½ red onion
- O 1 garlic clove
- O 2 sage leaves
- O 1 sprig thyme
- O 40 g (1½ oz) butter
- O 5 blue crabs
- O ½ bunch coriander (cilantro)
- O 500 g (1 lb 2 oz) good-quality puff pastry
- O Flour, for working the dough
- O 100 g (3½ oz) sour cream
- O 100 ml (3½ fl oz) white wine
- O 20 ml (¾ fl oz) pastis

Peel the potato and boil in salted water until soft. Then cut into 1 cm (½ inch) dice.

Peel onion and garlic and finely dice. Pluck sage leaves from the stems and finely chop. Pluck thyme leaves as well.

Melt 20 g (¾ oz) butter in a frying pan, add the chopped onion, garlic and potato and sauté until golden brown. Add the herbs.

Crack the crab shells and pick out the meat from the body and the claws. Finely chop coriander leaves. Add the crab meat and coriander to the pan and chill in the refrigerator.

Preheat oven to 220°C (425°F). Lay the puff pastry on a work surface dusted with flour, roll out and cut into 5 cm (2 inch) squares. Cut 1 cm (½ inch) wide strips from some of the squares and lay them like a frame around each of the remaining pastry squares.

Place the puff pastry on a baking tray lined with baking paper and distribute the crab filling evenly in the centre of each square. Spoon sour cream over the top. Bake in the oven until golden brown, about 15 minutes.

Pour white wine and pastis into a saucepan and reduce for 2–3 minutes. Add 20 g (¾ oz) butter, stir well and remove the pan from the heat.

Take the crab burekas out of the oven and serve immediately with the sauce.

HUNTER
Yale
MUL-T-LOCK
MAGNUM
ALBA

MAGNUM M1
SL64P
MAGNUM
Yale

FISH-EGGPLANT KOFTAS

For 3–4 people as an appetiser

- O 1 large roasted eggplant (aubergine (page 36)
- O 500 g (1 lb 2 oz) branzino fillet
- O 2 small onions
- O 3 garlic cloves
- O 5 acri sivri (cayenne) pepper
- O 15 g (½ oz) flat-leaf parsley
- O 30 g (1 oz) coriander (cilantro)
- O 1 heaped teaspoon sea salt
- O Olive oil, for frying
- O 2 tomatoes
- O 4 tablespoons Greek yoghurt

Scoop out the pulp from the roasted eggplant and drain in a sieve for at least 2 hours. Then squeeze the pulp between your hands to remove any remaining liquid.

Dice the branzino fillet very finely. Peel the onions and garlic and finely chop. Deseed 1 sivri pepper and finely dice; pluck herb leaves from the stems and finely chop. (You can also coarsely chop everything and put it through a meat grinder.) Place the chopped ingredients, along with the eggplant, in a bowl with the salt and knead well with your hands. Chill for 30 minutes in the refrigerator.

Rub your hands with olive oil, shape the chilled mixture into balls about 3–4 cm (1½ inches) in diameter and gently press flat. Put a large frying pan over high heat, add the olive oil and reduce the heat. Fry the koftas in the oil until crispy, about 3 minutes on each side. Halve the tomatoes and add to the pan along with the remaining sivri peppers and simmer for a few minutes.

Beat the yoghurt until creamy. Arrange the fish-eggplant koftas, tomatoes and sivri peppers on plates and serve with the yoghurt.

THE AESTHETE

MONTEFIORE 36
2752

RUTI BROUDO

R2M

»The Aesthete«

Ruti Broudo supposedly does not give many interviews, so we feel lucky to be sitting down with her at her soon-to-be-opened Japanese restaurant Herzl 16. Ruti is virtually a household name in Tel Aviv, thanks to her culinary ›empire‹. Her strength and determination do not surprise us, but we also find her to be somewhat shy and quickly realise that she is as interested in us as we are in her. It's no wonder that she says of herself: ›I am not particularly sociable, but I like hearing people's stories.‹

»It was so strange to charge money for serving food.«

A catalogue of Ruti's R2M, the 700-employee enterprise she runs with her business partner Mati, reads like its own food and hotel guide: CoffeeBar (the first place they opened), Brasserie M&R, Bakery (five locations), Hotel Montefiore (hotel and restaurant), Crème (ice cream shop), Delicatessen 79/81 (take-away and online orders), Café 12/Rothschild 12 (café and music bar) and Herzl 16, the latest addition.

Ruti's food and furnishings are not really Israeli. ›We bring other food cultures to Tel Aviv, and we are really about design and atmosphere,‹ she tells us. ›I am not carrying the flag of Israeli food.‹ When she returned to Tel Aviv from New York in 1994, she felt that a lot was missing here in terms of aesthetic and variety. And service. In this respect, she believes that there is still much room for improvement in Israel. As she says, ›People here are unique and smart but need to be much more considerate, especially of the environment‹.

Ruti's parents are Holocaust survivors, which greatly shaped her upbringing. She grew up in Netanya, north of Tel Aviv, in an orthodox family, and was sent to religious school along with her three siblings. Her father was secretly critical of religion but followed the rules, ›just in case there is a God‹. Great importance was placed on food in her family, which Ruti attributes to two factors: religion and the deprivations of the Holocaust. They observed every Shabbat, although for her it was often a tedious obligation. Her religious background even affected her initial business decisions: when she opened the CoffeeBar she was somewhat nervous about offering non-kosher food. But while she can appreciate the observance of holidays and traditions, she dislikes the rigidity of rules. She says that there is still always a certain conflict for her about it all.

Ruti's father ›lived‹ the holocaust every day and talked about it non-stop. As a consequence, Ruti describes the atmosphere at home as having been ›heavy‹, so she desperately wanted to leave.

She met Mati Broudo in the army and married him soon after. He was different: he had travelled a lot and had grown up partly in New York. She knew he would take her where she had always wanted to go. At just 21, she moved to New York with Mati to see the world. She was to stay for nine years and earn her living as a bookkeeper; however, for Ruti, New York in 1985 and the years following was about food and entertaining. She followed Martha Stewart and read countless home entertainment and design magazines. She and Mati hosted dinners for friends and, although they both did the cooking, the main focus was always on selecting the right music, paying attention to details of decor and offering just the right wines and spirits. They knew where to get everything. The seeds of Ruti's future career were planted during those New York years.

The concept for the CoffeeBar, their first business, came from a stopover in Italy on their way from New York to Israel. They opened it with the attitude that they had nothing to lose. They set up CoffeeBar in a somewhat industrial area and – contrary to all expectations – it was quite popular from the very beginning. Ruti recalls the first day as if it were yesterday: how nervous she was, especially because she felt it was so strange to charge money for serving food. The prices were so low they were nearly feeding the guests for free. People loved it and the place was packed every lunch time, but it didn't turn a profit.

Mati was critically important to the ultimate success of the business because he insisted they carry on when Ruti was almost ready to give up. They opened for dinner and the CoffeeBar became a real restaurant. For three years she was always there, handling everything, working around the clock. Mati supported her but travelled a great deal with his work and would always return with great new ideas.

The next major change in Ruti's life came in 1997, when Guy Polak, a shy and modest chef who had worked at Le Cordon Bleu, came to the CoffeeBar looking for a job. They hit it off and she hired him right away. With Guy in the kitchen, the place got great reviews and was full nearly every evening.

What came next? It was Mati who encouraged her to expand the business. December 2002 saw the opening of Brasserie M&R, today a very well-known French restaurant in the heart of the city. Ruti, Mati and Guy flew to Paris to prepare for it and wrote the menu on the plane. Ruti had already hired the best people to work there, Guy took over the kitchen, and the Brasserie was an immediate success. Today Guy is the head chef of the entire conglomerate and Ruti's life partner. She and Mati separated in 2012 but have remained business partners, and the three of them work together harmoniously.

Haya says of Ruti that she is known for being ›Europe in Tel Aviv‹. While Israel is often prone to balagan (an affectionate term for chaos or messiness), Ruti places great value on carefully thought-out details. She confesses with a smile that she does, indeed, take a lot of time to figure out just the right aesthetic for a place. She needs to approach the space step by step; she always has a notebook with her in which she makes sketches.

סוריה: טילים לא מכריעים מלחמות
CASIO
CASIO
MS-88

Everything in her restaurants is custom-designed, from the colour of the walls to the tableware. But although Ruti is somewhat of a perfectionist, she also readily collaborates with others and is happy to hear suggestions.

R2M's projects developed at a dizzying pace. The Hotel Montefiore was Mati's idea. Someone showed them the beautiful building and they were sold on it immediately. As is Ruti's style, there is great attention to detail: here she drew on colonial style for the décor. Today the Montefiore has become one of the best-known hotels and restaurants in all of Tel Aviv. At Delicatessen 79/81, a NY-style deli shop and restaurant, customers can order in advance online and then enjoy the food at home with their family. Every branch of the Bakery is managed by women. ›Women do service better than men,‹ says Ruti. The ice cream place, Crème, located at a busy part of Dizengoff Street, uses only fresh ingredients and serves only four flavours. Soon a production facility will open, a behind-the-scenes space intended to centralise much of the food production work.

In a few years, Ruti would like to retire, to spend more time in her beautiful home right next to the Carmel Market. She also loves to knit and travel. Ruti is proud of what she has accomplished and of her decisions, which were always well thought-out. As she says with a wink: ›After all, I'm responsible. As a woman, that's just who I am.‹

Ruti eventually helped her parents move to Tel Aviv. In spite of the difficulties in her youth, she still faithfully goes to her parents' home every Friday night for Shabbat dinner; however now, Ruti tells us, ›Shabbat is a pleasure and a meaningful tradition for me.‹ She adds: ›How life changes.‹

BEEF TARTARE BRUSCHETTA

RECIPE FROM RUTI BROUDO

For 4 people as an appetiser

For the Ancho aioli:

- O 1 egg yolk
- O 1 garlic clove
- O 50 ml (1½ fl oz) sriracha sauce
- O 1 teaspoon ancho chilli powder
- O Sea salt
- O 250 ml (9 fl oz) grape seed oil

For the radish-fennel salad:

- O 8 radishes
- O 1 fennel bulb
- O 8 miniature lettuce hearts
- O Olive oil
- O Lemon juice

For the Jerusalem artichoke chips:

- O 4 Jerusalem artichokes
- O Canola oil, for deep-frying

- O 4 slices sourdough bread
- O Olive oil
- O 1 handful flat-leaf parsley leaves
- O 400 g (14 oz) beef fillet
- O Lemon juice

For the *aioli*, purée all ingredients except the oil with a stick blender. Slowly pour in the oil in a thin stream, continuing to blend until you have a creamy, homogeneous mixture.

For the *salad*, cut or shave the radishes and fennel into very thin slices. Pull apart the lettuce hearts, mix with the radishes and fennel and marinate in the olive oil and lemon juice.

For the *Jerusalem artichoke chips*, peel the Jerusalem artichokes and cut into thin slices. Heat the oil in a deep saucepan to 175°C (350°F), add the sliced artichokes and deep-fry until golden brown. Remove from the oil with a mesh skimmer and drain on paper towels.

Brush the bread with olive oil and toast in a hot chargrill pan. Chop the parsley. Chop the meat very finely and mix with 4 tablespoons aioli, parsley and a dash of lemon juice. Immediately place on the warm bread, garnish with the chips and serve with the radish-fennel salad.

HAYA'S TIP:
YOU CAN REPLACE THE SRIRACHA SAUCE WITH A DESEEDED RED CHILLI PEPPER.

MARINATED ANCHOVIES WITH FENNEL GREENS, CHILLI & TOMATO SEEDS

RECIPE FROM RUTI BROUDO

For 4 people as an appetiser

For the marinated anchovies:

- O 12 fresh anchovy fillets
- O Sea salt
- O 1 lemon
- O 4 garlic cloves
- O 1 bird's eye chilli
- O 5 sprigs thyme
- O 200 ml (7 fl oz) olive oil
- O 30 ml (1 fl oz) lemon juice

- O 1 handful cherry tomatoes
- O Sea salt
- O Olive oil
- O Lemon juice
- O Fennel greens, to garnish
- O 2 tablespoons green aioli (page 143)

Rinse the anchovies well and carefully blot dry inside and out. Measure out the salt at 15 g (½ oz) per 100 g (3½ oz) anchovies and spread over a baking tray. Place the anchovies on the salt, skin side down. Chill for 2 hours.

Halve the lemon lengthways and cut into thin slices. Peel and finely chop the garlic. Deseed the chilli and cut into thin strips. Pluck the thyme leaves from the stems. Mix everything together with the olive oil and lemon juice, lay the anchovies in the marinade and chill for at least 12 hours.

Make a criss-cross cut in the skin on the bottom of each cherry tomato. Bring salted water (1 teaspoon salt per litre/35 fl oz water) to the boil in a saucepan, add the tomatoes and blanch for 1 minute. Immediately immerse the tomatoes in cold water and pull off the skin. Carefully squeeze the seeds from the tomatoes and set aside.

Remove the anchovies from the marinade, rinse again and blot dry. Arrange on plates with the skin side up and drizzle with a generous amount of olive oil and a bit of lemon juice. Garnish with the tomato seeds, skinned cherry tomatoes, fennel greens and a few drops of green aioli.

A crisp baguette is the perfect accompaniment to this dish.

MOROCCAN WEDDING SARDINES WITH TOMATO SALAD

For 4 people as an appetiser

For the tomato salad:
- 280 g (10 oz) tomatoes
- ¼ red onion
- ½ acri sivri (cayenne) pepper
- 1 wedge of an untreated lemon
- 2 sprigs coriander (cilantro)
- 4½ teaspoons olive oil
- Sea salt
- 4 tablespoons Greek yoghurt

For the sardines:
- 8 whole sardines, without scales, heads or bones
- 4 garlic cloves
- 20 g (¾ oz) coriander (cilantro)
- 20 g (¾ oz) flat-leaf parsley
- 2 slices pickled lemons (page 97)
- 4½ teaspoons harissa (page 95)
- 3 tablespoons olive oil
- Sea salt
- Plain flour, for dusting the sardines
- 4 tablespoons canola oil

HAYA'S TIP:
ASK THE FISH SELLER TO PREPARE THE SARDINES FOR YOU – THIS WILL SAVE YOU A LOT OF WORK, AS IT IS NOT AN EASY JOB.

For the *tomato salad,* dice the tomatoes and peel and finely dice the onion. Deseed the sivri pepper and cut into strips. Finely dice the lemon wedge with the peel. Pluck coriander leaves from the stems and finely chop. Mix together all ingredients except the yoghurt in a bowl, season with salt to taste and leave until it is to be used.

Cut the *sardines* lengthways on the belly side so that the fillets on the back are still attached and can be folded out like the wings of a butterfly and laid flat.

For the filling, peel and finely chop the garlic. Pluck the leaves of the herbs from the stems and chop them; finely chop pickled lemon as well. Combine the finely chopped ingredients with the harissa and olive oil and season to taste with salt. Spread the filling on the open surface of half of the sardines. Top with the remaining open sardines and dust them with flour.

Heat the oil in a large frying pan, add the sardines and fry until brown and crispy, 2–3 minutes per side.

Arrange sardines on plates. Add tomato salad and garnish with 1 tablespoon of yoghurt each.

Sardines m'joujine can be translated as ›married sardines‹. The connection between Morocco and weddings has a special meaning for us: while this book was being written, Nuriel and Audrey married in Marrakech. Nuriel knew from his first visit to Morocco – he did not yet have a girlfriend, so a wedding lay far in the future – that he would one day marry there. Audrey, as well, was enchanted from her very first visit. Even before the wedding planning really began, the location was settled: Morocco. And so we experienced a splendid wedding: family and friends travelled from many countries and the employees of the various NENI locations celebrated with us as well.

MEAT

FROM SHAWARMA TO CURRY

LAMB BUREKAS

For 4–6 people as a main dish

For the ragout:

- O 2 carrots
- O ¼ celeriac bulb
- O 2 onions
- O 1 acri sivri (cayenne) pepper
- O 5 tablespoons olive oil
- O 1 kg (2 lb 4 oz) boneless lamb shoulder
- O 750 ml (26 fl oz) white wine
- O ½ teaspoon crushed black pepper
- O 2 teaspoons sea salt
- O 1 sprig sage
- O 500 ml (17 fl oz) chicken broth (page 113)

- O 640 g (1 lb 6½ oz) frozen puff pastry (thawed slowly in the refrigerator)
- O 1 egg

For the sauce:

- O 6 spring onions (scallions)
- O 800 ml (28 fl oz) chicken broth (page 113)
- O 125 ml (4 fl oz) vermouth
- O 8 star anise
- O 160 g (5½ oz) butter

Preheat oven to 210°C (410°F). For the *ragout,* peel the carrots, celeriac and onions and cut into 5 mm (¼ inch) dice. Deseed the sivri pepper and finely dice. Heat 2 tablespoons olive oil in a flame-proof casserole, add the onions, carrots and celeriac and sauté until they get a little colour. Remove from the casserole and set aside.

Cut the lamb meat into 5 mm (¼ inch) pieces (nearly as small as ground meat). Heat 1 tablespoon olive oil in the casserole and sear a small amount of meat in it. (It is important to keep the meat in one layer and turn only when properly browned.) Remove the browned meat from the casserole and set aside on a plate. Brown the remaining meat in the same manner, adding 1 more tablespoon of oil each time. Finally, return all of the meat, with any juices, to the casserole and then add the white wine to deglaze the pot. Scrape up the bits from the bottom of the casserole with a wooden spoon.

Return the sautéed vegetables to the casserole and add all the remaining ingredients. Stir well and braise, covered, for 3 hours in the oven. →

Remove the ragout from the oven and keep warm on the stovetop over low heat. Reduce oven temperature to 190°C (375°F). Cut puff pastry sheets into 10 cm (4 inch) squares and place on a baking tray lined with baking paper. Beat egg with 50 ml (1½ fl oz) water and brush the dough with it. Bake the puff pastry in the oven until golden brown, about 25 minutes.

Meanwhile, for the *sauce*, trim away the dark green ends from the spring onions and cut into short lengths. Bring the chicken broth, vermouth, star anise and spring onions to the boil in a wide saucepan and cook until reduced to a third of the volume. Dice the butter, add to the pan and stir the sauce until it binds and takes on a lovely sheen.

To serve, carefully cut open the puff pastry squares. Arrange the ragout on the bottom sections of the pastry squares and cover with the lids. Drizzle several spoonfuls of sauce around the puff pastry and serve.

Burekas, a typical dish in the Middle East, originated in the Balkans. In Israel one can buy ready-made burekas that only need to be warmed in the oven. This is why they are popular as finger food when one has a lot of guests – which in Israel is nearly always the case. When it comes to the filling, you can let your imagination run wild: pumpkin seed oil and squash are an Austrian interpretation; ground meat with pine nuts comes from Persian cuisine; the combination of spinach and sheep's cheese is very popular in Turkey, while potatoes and onions are a variant with a Polish touch. The dough normally comes already filled, but at NENI the pastry is baked separately and serves as a ›lid‹ for slowly braised lamb.

HAYA'S TIPS:
THE RAGOUT CAN BE MADE A DAY IN ADVANCE AND REHEATED. THE LONG COOKING TIME ENSURES THE MEAT IS WONDERFULLY TENDER AND MERGES WITH THE OTHER FLAVOURS.

FOR A VEGETARIAN VERSION, I OFTEN FILL THE PUFF PASTRY WITH ROASTED EGGPLANT (AUBERGINE), TAHINI (PAGE 94) AND A LITTLE GRATED SHEEP'S CHEESE.

DUCK–TAMARIND CURRY WITH FRIED EGGPLANT

For 4 people as a main dish

For the eggplant:
- O 3 eggplant (aubergines), about 1 kg (2 lb 4 oz)
- O 5 tablespoons olive oil
- O Sea salt

For the tamarind–curry paste:
- O 1½ teaspoons coriander seeds
- O ½ teaspoon cumin seeds
- O 2 French shallots
- O 8 garlic cloves
- O 15 g (½ oz) arrowroot starch
- O 40 g (1½ oz) fresh galangal
- O 1 lemongrass stalk
- O 1 bird's eye chilli
- O 45 g (1½ oz) dark palm sugar
- O 45 g (1½ oz) Thai basil
- O 2 tablespoons grape seed oil
- O 40 g (1½ oz) tamarind paste
- O 1 teaspoon fresh green peppercorns

For the duck:
- O 4 duck legs (about 1.5 kg/3 lb 5 oz)
- O 3 teaspoons sea salt

For the curry sauce:
- O 1 lemongrass stalk
- O 400 ml (14 fl oz) coconut milk
- O 630 ml (21 fl oz) chicken broth (page 113)
- O 4½ teaspoons fish sauce
- O 1 teaspoon sea salt
- O 1 teaspoon ground turmeric
- O 2 kaffir lime leaves

For the basil-coconut sauce:
- O ½ fresh turmeric root, or 1 teaspoon ground turmeric
- O 100 ml (3½ fl oz) coconut milk
- O 24 Thai basil leaves
- O Sea salt

→

HAYA'S TIPS:
I FREQUENTLY MAKE A LARGER AMOUNT OF CURRY PASTE AND USE IT FOR THAI VEGETABLE CURRIES OR COCONUT SOUPS. IT KEEPS IN THE REFRIGERATOR FOR SEVERAL WEEKS.

FRESH GREEN PEPPER IS AVAILABLE AT INDIAN OR ASIAN GROCERS. IF YOU CAN'T FIND IT, YOU CAN LEAVE IT OUT.

Preheat the oven to 140°C (275°F). Peel the *eggplant*, cut into 2.5 cm (1 inch) thick slices and place on a baking tray lined with baking paper. Brush with olive oil and season with salt. Bake for 90 minutes in the oven without turning. Set aside until you are ready to serve.

While the eggplant bakes, make the *curry paste:* dry-roast the coriander and cumin in a frying pan until they release their aromas. Peel the shallots, garlic, arrowroot starch and galangal. Remove the outer leaves and green parts from the lemongrass. Deseed chilli as desired (the curry is hotter with the seeds). Blitz all ingredients except the green peppercorns together with a blender to make a paste. Coarsely crush the green pepper and add.

Increase the oven temperature to 220°C (425°F). Season the *duck legs* with salt and coat with half the curry paste. Place the legs in an ovenproof dish, skin side down, and bake for 30 minutes. Turn and bake for another 15 minutes with the skin side up.

Meanwhile, for the *curry sauce,* remove outer leaves and green parts from the lemongrass and cut the inner part into 5 cm (2 inch) pieces. Bring to the boil in a saucepan with the remaining curry paste and all remaining ingredients. Simmer over medium heat until the liquid is reduced by about a quarter.

Pour the sauce over the precooked duck legs. Trim a piece of baking paper to fit the ovenproof dish and cover the duck with it. Bake for 1 more hour in the oven.

Meanwhile, for the *basil-coconut sauce,* peel the turmeric and cut into thin slices. Bring the coconut milk with the turmeric and Thai basil to the boil in a pan and cook until reduced by half. Season with salt to taste.

Remove duck from the oven. Pour a bit of the hot curry sauce over the eggplant and leave for a few minutes. Then arrange the eggplant on the plates, followed by the duck legs drizzled with the remaining sauce. Garnish with the basil-coconut sauce and serve with steamed rice.

A large number of Indian Jews live in Tel Aviv, which is why Indian food is so popular here. Today, even award-winning restaurants put on Indian evenings, and Indian street food is everywhere you look.

THE ETHICAL CARNIVORES

YARON KESTENBAUM & JONATHAN BOROWITZ

M25

»The Ethical Carnivores«

The restaurant M25 is a paradise for carnivores. It is located on a side street of the Carmel Market, just 25 metres away from the Meat Market butchery, also owned by the group; hence the name. We sit at one of the few simple tables facing the street. Through the entrance we can see the glass display case inside in which various kinds of meats are perfectly arranged. Here the customers can choose their preferred cut. The bustling restaurant is connected to a quiet garden. In the kitchen, everything is immaculate and perfectly organised.

While opening a restaurant for carnivores might not be in keeping with today's trends, M25 has nonetheless become one of Tel Aviv's top restaurants. This success can be attributed to the fortuitous coming together of responsible and dedicated partners, environmental consciousness, clear guiding principles, creativity and a passionate team spirit. What a stroke of luck for the guests!

We meet Yaron, one of the three founders of M25. At twenty he began training as a cook, worked with top chefs like Alain Ducasse and now has over thirty years of experience in the restaurant business. Joining us at the table is Jonathan, head chef and responsible for operations. He previously studied political science in New York, worked for a time as assistant to the Israeli Minister of Finance and spent six years at the French Culinary Institute. Another fixture of the team is Michal, the restaurant's manager. She and Yaron planned the restaurant together. Their design combines a market-like ambience with a modern, laid-back atmosphere.

In our conversation with Yaron and Jonathan, the ambition of M25 and the affiliated businesses becomes clear: educating people about meat. The Meat Market butchery opened in 2013 with the aim of providing the best local beef in Tel Aviv. When the restaurant opened two years later, 300 customers came the first day. The clientele was – and still is – very diverse. Jonathan says that wealthy people mostly want steak but also recalls a woman who just ordered two green salads, so obviously discerning vegetarians can also find something to their liking here. On a Friday afternoon, sometimes between 250 and 280 people eat here in the space of about four hours.

Based on his long experience, Yaron developed some fundamental principles for M25. He is very knowledgeable about the meat industry in Israel and knew that he could achieve his goals only by working hand in hand with an exceptionally dedicated cattle farmer. It took three years until he found the right one, near Ashkelon.

»Take meat only from an animal that was properly raised, and accept only the best quality.«

The handling of the animals is crucial to the quality of the meat. Every step in the process – from the raising of the cattle to the final sale or to the serving of the finished dish in the restaurant – is closely monitored. M25 decided to raise Holsteins, originating in the Netherlands, and Simmentaler, which are very popular in Belgium and Germany. The quality of feed for their cows also has a direct impact on the flavour of the meat. In Israel, natural grass is available only four months of the year, so the rest of the time the feed is a carefully composed mixture of fruits and vegetables. M25's kitchen follows the ›nose to tail‹ philosophy, using every part of the animal. For example, they serve smoked sweetbreads on a salad or tongue as a delicious appetiser. Not wasting anything shows respect for the animal.

So how can one recognise a good steak? Yaron recommends checking the general appearance of the meat, its marbling and outside fat, and asking how the animal was raised. The animal's age depends on individual preference and food culture. Ideally, M25 does not use meat from calves but rather that of cows at least two years old. There is virtually no maximum age here; recently the winning meat at a steak competition came from a fifteen-year-old cow in Galicia!

Initially Yaron was in charge of the food at M25, and then Jonathan took over as head chef. It was obvious to us from the very first moment why these two make such a successful team: Yaron prefers purity and simplicity in his recipes and on the plates – moderate seasoning, superbly prepared meat, a little bit of green and maybe a little aioli. In following these principles, Jonathan's style evolved toward an even greater simplicity. He compares the use of fewer ingredients to the challenge faced by a painter who can choose from only five colours for a picture. A perfect duo!

But cooking simply is not always easy. Making perfect shawarma, for example, is a two-day process. Lamb and beef are first marinated, smoked slightly, and only then grilled. All ingredients must be carefully selected, from the best olive oil to the homemade lemon paste, and the temperature of the heavy charcoal grill must remain constant at all times.

An Arabic and Sephardic concept has a special significance at M25: shipudia. Shipud means a skewer but also refers to a place with a grill; it implies socialising, outside tables, backgammon games, hookah – in short, a lifestyle with a North African flavour. For Jonathan, this is what he wants to achieve at M25. And as it so often happens, the spirit of this place, as well, showed itself best in a crisis: one busy evening with a full house there was suddenly a total electricity failure. But instead of all the guests being sent home, the cooks continued working by the light of their mobile phones, candles were placed on the tables, the service staff improvised, and not one customer got up and left. M25 assumed the cost for all the food. ›This place is a miracle‹ was the verdict of one customer.

Both Yaron and Jonathan are politically and socially engaged people, often critical of Israel and worrying that the country is going in the wrong direction. Jonathan is active in refugee work, raising funds and organising events, some of them at M25. He feels that he reaches more people this way than he did in his former government job. Yaron speaks of plans to open a branch of M25 in an underprivileged area of Israel.

We have now worked up an appetite and go into the garden to eat. Here we find an oasis of tranquillity in the bustling market area. We can select meat from the display cases or order from the menu. Jonathan recommends that we first try the *arayes* (pita filled with lamb) and then a steak. We also decide on shawarma, kebabs, tongue, corned beef, sweetbreads and fresh salads, all of which soon arrive on our long table. We love everything and agree that the whole team here and the wonderful atmosphere represent the epitome of genuine shipudia!

ARAYES

RECIPE FROM YARON KESTENBAUM AND JONATHAN BOROWITZ

For 4 people as a main dish

- 500 g (1 lb 2 oz) aged beef (from the shoulder or entrecôte)
- 100 g (3½ oz) lamb fat
- 2 onions
- 1 handful flat-leaf parsley leaves
- 2 teaspoons sea salt
- 1 teaspoon black pepper
- 4 pita breads
- Olive oil, for frying

Preheat the oven to 220°C (425°F). Put beef and lamb fat through the meat grinder together (or have your butcher grind it for you). Peel and finely chop onions. Finely chop parsley. Combine in a large bowl with the meat, salt and pepper and knead together thoroughly.

Halve the pitas and fill each with an eighth of the meat filling. Heat olive oil in a frying pan, add the stuffed pitas and fry them for 3 minutes on each side. Transfer to the hot oven and let rest for 5 minutes.

Remove stuffed pitas from the oven and halve the pieces. Serve with tomato salad (page 180) and tahini (page 94).

HAYA'S TIP:
IF YOU DON'T LIKE THE STRONG FLAVOUR OF LAMB, REPLACE PART OF THE LAMB FAT WITH MINCED BEEF.

SHAKSHUKA WITH MERGUEZ

For 4–6 people for breakfast

- 1 kg (2 lb 4 oz) tomatoes
- 1 acri sivri (cayenne) pepper
- 6 garlic cloves
- 5–6 tablespoons olive oil
- 4 hot merguez, salsiccia or chorizo sausages
- Sea salt
- 6 eggs
- Fresh herbs, such as flat-leaf parsley, coriander (cilantro) and basil
- Focaccia (page 93) or sourdough bread, to serve

Cut out the stems of the tomatoes and make crisscross incisions on their bases. Bring salted water (1 teaspoon salt per litre/35 fl oz water) to the boil in a saucepan and blanch the tomatoes in it for 1 minute. Immediately immerse in iced water, pull off the skin and quarter the skinned tomatoes. Cut tomatoes into 3 cm (1¼ inch) cubes.

Halve the sivri pepper lengthways, deseed and cut into small dice. Peel garlic and finely dice as well.

Heat the olive oil in a large frying pan and sear the merguez. Remove from the pan to a plate. Place the sivri in the pan and sauté for 1 minute. Add the garlic and sauté for 1 more minute. Add the cubed tomatoes, season with salt and continue to sauté over high heat until the tomatoes are soft. Scrape the pan frequently with a wooden spoon to loosen any bits from the base.

Return the merguez to the pan. Make 6 wells in the mixture with a spoon and break an egg into each. Cover and cook over low heat until the egg whites begin to firm but the yolks are still runny.

Cut the herbs into very thin strips and scatter over the shakshuka. Serve with toasted bread.

HAYA'S TIP:
LIKE THE GREEN SHAKSHUKA (PAGE 49), THIS RECIPE CAN ALSO BE PREPARED IN INDIVIDUAL PORTIONS IN SMALL PANS.

Shawarma is familiar as the doner from Turkish cuisine. This meat, typically grilled on a vertical rotisserie, is widespread. Along with falafel and sabich (page 88), it is the most common Israeli street food. This recipe is a homage to the food of the streets of Tel Aviv.

CHICKEN SHAWARMA

For 4 people as a main dish

For the chicken:

- O 25 g (1 oz) fresh turmeric, or 1 tablespoon ground turmeric
- O 10 garlic cloves
- O 1 fresh red chilli
- O 1 tablespoon cumin seeds
- O 1 tablespoon sea salt
- O 1 teaspoon black pepper
- O 80 ml (2½ fl oz) lemon juice
- O 125 ml (4 fl oz) olive oil
- O 2 red onions
- O 4 chicken legs (with skin, without bones)
- O 2 sprigs thyme
- O 2 cinnamon sticks

For the herb salad:

- O ½ bunch flat-leaf parsley
- O ½ bunch coriander (cilantro)
- O ½ bunch mint
- O 1 acri sivri (cayenne) pepper
- O ½ bunch spring onions (scallions, green parts only)
- O 1 tablespoon olive oil
- O 1 tablespoon lemon juice
- O Sea salt

- O 4 slices sourdough bread
- O Double recipe of garlic cream (page 18)

HAYA'S TIP:
BE SURE TO BEGIN MARINATING THE MEAT IN GOOD TIME SO THE MARINADE CAN PERMEATE THE MEAT.

For the *chicken,* peel turmeric and garlic and coarsely dice. Halve the chilli and deseed if you like. Dry-roast the cumin in a small pan until fragrant. With a stick blender or in a blender, blitz the chilli, salt, pepper, lemon juice, turmeric, cumin, garlic and olive oil to make a smooth marinade.

Peel onions and cut into 5 mm (¼ inch) wide strips. Put the chicken legs, onion strips, thyme, cinnamon and marinade in a bowl, mix well, cover with plastic wrap and leave for 4 hours or overnight in the refrigerator.

Preheat oven to 200°C (400°F). Place chicken in an ovenproof dish along with the marinade and bake, skin side down, for 10 minutes. Turn the chicken and leave in the oven for 10 minutes. Increase the oven to 220°C (425°F) and cook the legs under the oven's grill until the meat is done and the skin is very crispy, about 10 more minutes.

Meanwhile, for the *salad,* pluck the herbs from the stems. Halve the sivri pepper lengthways, deseed and finely dice. Trim the spring onion greens and cut into very thin strips. Place everything in a bowl. Just before serving, stir together with the olive oil, lemon juice and salt to taste.

Toast the sourdough bread and spread with the garlic cream. Remove chicken from the oven, coarsely chop and arrange on the bread. Garnish with the herb salad and serve immediately.

In Israel, cabbage and meat are often prepared as an upside-down dish instead of as meat-filled sarma rolls. It is less work than stuffing the filling into the little rolls – and is very attractive on the table as well.

MAQLUBA

For 4–6 people as a main dish

- O 700 g (1 lb 9 oz) shoulder of lamb (without fat)
- O Sea salt
- O 1 flat-head cabbage, as young as possible (Jaroma variety)
- O 180 ml (6 fl oz) olive oil
- O 700 g (1 lb 9 oz) onions
- O 1 heaped teaspoon hot curry powder
- O 1 heaped teaspoon ground cumin
- O 1 heaped teaspoon baharat spice mix
- O 500 g (1 lb 2 oz) tomatoes
- O 7 garlic cloves
- O 250 g (9 oz) short-grain rice
- O Sour cream, to serve

For the gremolata:

- O ½ bunch flat-leaf parsley
- O 1 acri sivri (cayenne) pepper
- O 4 tablespoons olive oil
- O 2 tablespoons sherry vinegar, or any mild vinegar
- O 180 ml (6 fl oz) lemon juice
- O Sea salt

Cut lamb into 7 cm (2–3 inch) cubes. Place in a large saucepan, add plenty of water to cover and bring to the boil. Simmer meat for 1 hour without salt, then add 1 teaspoon salt and simmer another 30 minutes. Constantly skim off any foam collecting on the surface.

While the lamb simmers, preheat oven to 240°C (475°F). Bring an ample amount of salted water to the boil in a large saucepan. Place the whole cabbage head in the water and cook for about 10 minutes, then remove from the water and let cool a bit. Quarter the cabbage without cutting all the way through, so that it holds together at the stalk and the leaves open like a flower. Place on a roasting tin lined with baking paper and rub 3 tablespoons olive oil and 1 tablespoon salt thoroughly into the cabbage so each leaf is coated. Cover with foil and bake for about 15 minutes, then remove the foil and roast until golden brown, another 5 minutes. Take out and set aside.

Peel the onions and cut roughly into rings. Warm 3 tablespoons of olive oil in a large ovenproof saucepan over low heat, add the onions and slowly sauté for 15–20 minutes to allow them to release their sweetish aroma.

Add the curry powder, cumin and baharat to the onions and stir in 2 tablespoons of the cooking water from the lamb. Set aside in the pan until needed.

Cut out the stems of the tomatoes and make crisscross incisions in the skin on the bases. Bring salted water (1 teaspoon of salt per litre/35 fl oz water) to the boil in a saucepan, add the tomatoes and blanch for 1 minute. Immediately immerse in iced water, pull off the skin and cut the skinned tomatoes into wedges.

Peel and finely chop the garlic. Warm 3 tablespoons of olive oil in a frying pan over low heat, add the garlic and tomatoes and gently sauté for several minutes.

Preheat oven to 220°C (425°F). Remove the cooked lamb from the water (reserving the water) and add to the onions in the pan. Add the tomatoes as well and mix thoroughly. Braise, uncovered, for 20 minutes in the oven.

Meanwhile, wash the rice in a sieve until the water runs almost clear. Boil in the lamb cooking water until soft, 20–25 minutes, and strain.

Increase oven temperature to 240°C (475°F). Layer half of the cabbage evenly in a senia or a large, non-stick frying pan, followed by the rice, and then the meat. Finish with the remaining cabbage, pressing the layers together a bit so that they hold together well. Return to the oven for another 10–15 minutes.

Meanwhile, for the *gremolata,* pluck the parsley leaves from their stems and coarsely chop. Deseed the sivri pepper and finely dice. Combine with olive oil, vinegar, lemon juice and 2 tablespoons water and season to taste with salt.

Unmould the maqluba onto a large plate and serve with sour cream and the gremolata.

HAYA'S TIP:
THE MAQLUBA CAN ALSO BE MADE IN A SPRING-FORM TIN AND CUT INTO PIECES AFTER IT IS COOKED.

SLOW-BRAISED OXTAIL

For 4 people as a main dish

- O 1.5 kg (3 lb 5 oz) oxtail, sliced
- O 2 tablespoons olive oil
- O Sea salt
- O Black pepper
- O 1 litre (35 fl oz) red wine
- O 3 sprigs thyme
- O 3 bay leaves
- O 75 g (2½ oz) butter
- O 1 spring onion (scallion), green parts only
- O 4 small round breads or 1 large focaccia (page 93)

HAYA'S TIP:
SLOW-BRAISED MEAT IS WONDERFULLY TENDER AND GROWS MORE FLAVOURFUL THE LONGER IT COOKS. THE PREPARATION IS VERY SIMPLE: YOU JUST HAVE TO REMEMBER TO START IN GOOD TIME.

Rub the oxtail with the olive oil and 1 teaspoon each of salt and pepper. Heat a very large saucepan, add the meat and brown until it takes on colour. Deglaze with the red wine and add the thyme and bay leaves. Cover and simmer over low heat until the meat falls off the bone, about 6 hours. Add a bit of water as needed; the meat should always be covered with liquid. Frequently skim off any fat that collects on the surface.

Remove the meat from the pan and set aside. Boil the liquid over high heat until it has reduced to about 200 ml (7 fl oz). Stir in the butter, and season the sauce to taste with salt and pepper. Return the meat to the pan and briefly warm in the sauce.

To serve, trim the green part of the spring onions into very thin strips. Arrange the braised oxtail with the sauce on the bread and garnish with the sliced spring onions.

GLAZED SHORT RIBS

For 4 people as a main dish

For the meat:

- O 300 g (10½ oz) sea salt
- O 300 g (10½ oz) sugar
- O 1.2 kg (2 lb 10 oz) beef short ribs without bones, or 1.6 kg (3 lb 8 oz) ribs with bones

For the glaze:

- O 40 g (1½ oz) maple syrup
- O 40 g (1½ oz) white miso paste
- O 50 g (1¾ oz) harissa (page 95)
- O 50 g (1¾ oz) pickled lemons (page 97)
- O 50 ml (1½ fl oz) olive oil

- O 3 carrots
- O 2 small cucumbers
- O 1 red onion
- O 1 lime
- O 1 acri sivri (cayenne) pepper
- O 1 fresh red chilli
- O 200 g (7 oz) squash harissa (page 122)
- O Several sprigs of coriander (cilantro)
- O Bread, to serve, such as leek buns (page 59), lahoh (page 216) or focaccia (page 93)

For the *meat,* mix together the salt and sugar in a large bowl, add the meat and thoroughly massage it with the salt-sugar mixture. Cover with plastic wrap and leave overnight in the refrigerator.

Preheat the oven to 170°C (340°F). Wash meat and thoroughly blot dry with a paper towel. Place in an ovenproof dish, cover with foil and roast in the oven for 3 hours.

Meanwhile, for the *glaze,* blitz all ingredients with a stick blender or in a blender to makea paste.

Peel the carrots and cut into thin strips. Cut the cucumbers into thin strips as well. Peel the onion and cut into half rings. Cut the lime into wedges. Deseed the sivri pepper and chilli as desired and finely slice.

Increase the oven temperature to 220°C (425°F). Remove the meat, brush with glaze and then return to the oven to roast for 5–10 minutes. Remove from the oven and carefully pull the meat from the bones.

Serve the meat with squash harissa, vegetable sticks, pepper, chilli, coriander and bread.

HAYA'S TIP:
I LIKE TO PUT ALL THE INGREDIENTS ON THE TABLE SEPARATELY SO THAT EVERYONE CAN BUILD THEIR OWN INDIVIDUAL SANDWICH.

לתעודה

THE SPICE MERCHANT

ARIE HABSHUSH

Arie Habshush Spices Herbs Ltd
»The Spice Merchant«

»Habshush means ›loved by the people‹.«

We had already heard so much about the Habshush spice shop at the Levinsky Market, an almost mythical culinary meeting place in Tel Aviv. But finding it turned out to be not all that easy. On that bustling street we see many shops, most of them with no name or sign. Our sense of smell leads us to a green, graffiti-covered metal door. There is apparently no need for any kind of special sign because every good chef in Tel Aviv knows what he will find here.

As we enter the narrow, crowded shop we first encounter Arie, the patriarch, who sits behind the old-fashioned cash register on the left by the entrance while two of his sons and a father-in-law of one of them arrange goods. The storeroom is filled with countless sacks of freshly ground spices, and between them narrow passages lead to shelves of more spices, boxes, and perfectly arranged pyramids of chewing tobacco rolls. In the back area are two ancient spice grinders – reminders of the company's origins. Habshush remains to this day a family business. Like at NENI, everyone here has his field of activity; all tasks are equally valuable and are carried out with care and respect. Arie is always on hand to advise the customers, his sons Ori and Itamar see to the processing of the spices, and their mother Daliah is responsible for the ordering and the deliveries to the restaurants of Tel Aviv.

Elihay can still clearly recall his first year as a cook in Tel Aviv, when he was not yet very knowledgeable about spices and even occasionally forgot an order. He could always count on the support of the Habshush family; they advised him with boundless patience, brought every delivery punctually and helped him forge contacts with other chefs. Arie and his family know all their customers by name and take time for all of their concerns. Nothing here is done ›on the quick‹, which is perhaps also a reason that many elderly people shop here. Haya finds a suitable description for the shop: ›It is the last island in Tel Aviv. Here everything is just how it used to be.‹

The history of the spice business is long, and that of this family as well. The name Habshush can be translated as ›loved by the people‹ and comes from Ottoman times. It is an apt name for these friendly and patient people. The Habshushes were originally a wealthy Jewish family in Yemen who lent money and for over 200 years worked in the spice trade in Sana'a. Arabic was spoken at home and everyone learned Hebrew by reading the Torah. As a spice merchant, Arie's father travelled the world, arriving in Palestine for the first time in 1927 to explore the possibility of moving his spice business there. Although the prospects were not encouraging, the family emigrated in 1931 and opened a shop at a market near the port of Jaffa.

Arie was born in 1947. These were difficult times for Jews in Jaffa, and the family ultimately moved to Tel Aviv – to the location where they have remained to this day. Arie's kindergarten and school were right next to the shop, and the family

COCOMI BIO
ORGANIC COCONUT
FLOUR

lived on the third floor of the building. Later, the neighbourhood changed: more and more Persian and Iraqi immigrants were setting up shops and the Yemenite community moved to the Carmel Market. The Habshush family was the only Yemenite merchant to remain at the Levinsky Market. Today the business maintains state-of-the-art facilities on the outskirts of the city for receiving goods and for mixing and grinding spices. The decision to stay in this simple space is a sign of respect for Arie's father.

Arie crosses the street with us and shows us the small storeroom there, where we sit in a small cleared space between sacks of spices. Daliah, the matriarch of the family, has prepared a variety of small dishes for us. Arie's wife is a vivacious and elegant woman who tells us her own impressive family history: she comes from one of only two families in Israel that have never been expelled from their homeland. The Hasan and Zinati families have lived here for over forty generations and trace their roots back to ancient Canaan. Daliah smiles at her husband: ›He likes antiques.‹

Daliah's food complements our interview perfectly: two spicy soups, spreads and fresh bread. We sample the Yemenite *hilbe*, a specialty made with fresh fenugreek mixed with lemon and coriander. Meanwhile, Arie and Ori describe the development of the best and gentlest cold grinding techniques for spices, declaring that they would never use cheap fillers! Freshly ground cardamom and a bag of fragrant za'atar are passed around for us to smell. We begin wondering whether we can ever buy spices anywhere else again.

Like his father before him, Arie travels a lot on business to India, Turkey and many African countries. He never buys large amounts at a time because spices are delicate and many need to be ground no more than three months after purchase. In their warehouses outside the city, they use state-of-the-art Peruzzo hammer mills to do this. This is also where experiments are done and new mixtures are created. Many ideas come from chefs with whom they are friends.

In this global business, Arie allows his sons to make changes. Ori, friendly and outgoing, has clearly inherited the passion for the business: even as a baby he and his three siblings were surrounded by the fragrance of spices. After the army, he studied graphic design but could not see himself spending his life in front of a computer. His father needed help but warned him that this was a difficult business. The decision to run the business together, however, turned out to be the right one: Ori loves the customers and they love him.

He raves about the best Indian halva and the health benefits of spices: the antiseptic qualities of turmeric, the antioxidant properties of black pepper, the digestive benefits of cumin seeds and the cholesterol-lowering effect of fenugreek. Older customers often tell of mystical properties of certain spices passed down throughout history. Ori likes to describe the spice trade as a kind of pharmacy and sees himself as something of a pharmacist for whom spices are ›food to keep your body in shape‹.

Four years ago Ori's younger brother Itamar joined the business as well. The family has no great plans for expansion. ›We do not need a Porsche,‹ says Ori. If he were not so busy, he would love to offer courses and pass on his knowledge of spices. We were able to enjoy a taste of that. We could sit and chat for hours with the Habshushes, and we feel like old friends. But they have a lot to do and we have to move on as well. One thing has become clear during our visit: this remarkable family enterprise is an institution. And this is known by professional chefs as well as those who simply want some culinary advice or wish to immerse themselves for a while in the fragrant world of another age.

YEMENI BEEF STEW WITH LAHOH

RECIPE FROM DALIAH HABSHUSH

For 4–6 people as a main dish

For the hulba:
- O 2 teaspoons ground fenugreek
- O ½ teaspoon salt
- O 1 teaspoon zhug (page 95), plus extra to serve

For the stew:
- O 1 kg (2 lb 4 oz) shoulder of beef (fresh or hung)
- O 1 large onion
- O 1 bunch spring onions (scallions)
- O 1 bunch mint
- O 3 tablespoons ghee or olive oil
- O 1 heaped tablespoon soup hawaij
- O 1 tablespoon sea salt

For the lahoh:
- O 730 g (1 lb 9 oz) tepid water
- O 15 g (½ oz) sugar
- O 25 g (1 oz) dried yeast
- O 500 g (1 lb 2 oz) plain flour
- O 30 g (1 oz) semolina
- O 10 g (¼ oz) salt
- O Canola oil, for frying

For the *hulba,* soak the fenugreek for 3 hours in three times as much water, changing the water every hour to take out the bitterness. (Hold back the fenugreek with a plate when you drain the water.)

While the fenugreek soaks, make the *stew:* Cut the meat in 2 cm (¾ inch) cubes. Peel and coarsely chop the onion. Trim and finely chop the spring onions. Pluck the mint leaves from the stems and chop as well.

Heat the ghee in a stockpot, add the onion and sauté until transparent. Add the cubed beef and continue to cook. Add half of the spring onions and mint, cover and simmer over low heat for 1 hour.

Add the hawaij spices and salt and stir in the remaining spring onions and mint leaves. Pour in 250 ml (9 fl oz) of boiling water and simmer the stew for 1 more hour.

While the meat cooks, combine all the ingredients for the *lahoh* except the oil and stir until smooth. Leave to rise until doubled in size, about 1 hour.

Heat a small amount of oil in a non-stick frying pan, then wipe out with paper towel. Pour 1 ladle of the batter into the pan and tip back and forth to spread evenly. Cook over medium heat until small bubbles form and the batter is golden brown and dry. Do not turn. Take out of the pan and keep warm in the oven until ready to serve. Cook the rest of the batter in the same way; between batches, cool the pan with water if needed.

Drain the water one last time from the soaked fenugreek and beat with a fork or a mixer until white and creamy, rather like mayonnaise. Add a bit of water as needed, and season with salt and zhug.

Season the stew with salt to taste and serve with the lahoh, zhug and hulba.

HAYA'S TIPS:

HULBA HAS AN INTENSIVE AND SPICY AROMA. IT IS VERY HEALTHY AND IS SAID TO HELP PURIFY THE KIDNEYS. IT GOES WELL WITH SOUPS, TOMATO SALAD AND TAHINI, OR JUST DIP FRESH BREAD IN IT. ADD A SQUIRT OF LEMON JUICE IF YOU LIKE – MY HUSBAND, SAMY, LOVES IT THIS WAY.

THE MAGIC INGREDIENT IN THIS STEW IS THE YEMENI SPICE MIXTURE HAWAIJ, WHICH TRANSFORMS THE DISH INTO SOMETHING VERY SPECIAL. HAWAIJ USUALLY CONSISTS OF CUMIN, CARDAMOM, TURMERIC AND PEPPER AND IS USED TO SEASON RICE AND VEGETABLES AND AS A MARINADE FOR GRILLED FOODS.

LAMB WITH FIGS & GRAPES

For 6 people as a main dish

- O 250 g (9 oz) sea salt
- O 180 g (6¼ oz) sugar
- O 1.8 kg (4 lb) shoulder of lamb (with bones)
- O 250 ml (9 fl oz) chicken broth (page 113)
- O 400 g (14 oz) sweet red grapes, such as muscat
- O 8 fresh figs
- O 2 apples

Mix together the salt and sugar. Rub the shoulder of lamb all over with the mixture, place in a large ovenproof casserole and scatter the rest of the salt and sugar over the top. Cover and leave in the refrigerator for at least 4 hours or overnight.

Preheat oven to 190°C (375°F). Wash the lamb and blot dry. Place in a large deep roasting tin and pour the chicken broth over the top. Gently crush half the grapes with your hand and sprinkle over the lamb. Cover with foil and bake for 3½ hours. Occasionally scrape the roast drippings from the bottom of the tin and baste the lamb with the broth. Add a bit more water as needed.

Halve the figs, cut the apples into wedges and add to the meat with the remaining grapes. Bake for 1 more hour, uncovered; the lamb should be properly browned. Remove from the oven and lift the meat out of the roasting tin. Skim the fat from the cooking juices and serve the juices with the lamb and caramelised fruit.

HAYA'S TIP:
A GOOD SIDE DISH TO SERVE HERE IS JERUSALEM ARTICHOKES WITH FREEKEH (PAGE 31).

THE TRADITIONALIST

ELRAN SHREFLER

Azura Tel Aviv

»The Traditionalist«

An imposing figure of a man, Elran Shrefler runs his open kitchen at Azura with great commitment and a very personal style. The restaurant is an integral part of who he is. He greets us with a warm smile. It is still morning, several hours before lunch. From the kitchen come tempting aromas and large pots already sit atop individual small oil stoves, their contents simmering slowly: this is ›slow food‹ in the truest sense of the word. A woman is shaping meatballs and arranging them on a tray. She shows us moussaka, meat and cheese between thin slices of eggplant (aubergine), ready to go into the oven.

The original Azura was started in 1954 in Jerusalem by Elran's father and is a very well known and popular restaurant there. Like NENI, Azura is a family-run business. Whenever we visit Jerusalem, we eat there; the restaurant, located in the Iraqi part of the Machane Yehuda Market, offers the best food in the area. We're of course happy that there is now an Azura in Tel Aviv and through our conversation with Elran, we discover that it is not simply a continuation of the family tradition, but rather a new beginning. Located on a street corner not far from Rothschild Boulevard, it is housed in a beautiful old worn building with an airy and sunny glassed-in veranda. Immediately adjacent is a huge construction pit whose barriers are appropriately decorated with posters showing images of food. Towering behind the construction site are the high-rises of central Tel Aviv, where another world begins.

The kitchen and indoor seating area, an open plan creating one large room, is designed with an eclectic mix of restored brick walls, beautifully coloured tiles and industrial lamps. An old white wall, adorned with a massive Turkish flag of Atatürk looking sternly down, provides an iconic sense of another place and time. The restaurant, both indoor and veranda, is at once minimalist and warm, so far one of our favourite places to sit!

Elran accompanies us to the veranda, coffee in hand. He speaks animatedly about his father, who is a central influence in his life, and the place his father came from: Diyarbakir in Kurdish Turkey, close to the Iraqi border. Diyarbakir is at the heart of the family culinary traditions, along with the nearby city of Urfa (Şanlıurfa). Elran says this area has the ›best food in the world‹. Elran is the youngest of nine brothers and sisters. Even as a young boy, he spent much of his time in the kitchen and always wanted to emulate his father. His father was constantly in the kitchen; so was he. His father drinks whisky; so does Elran.

Elran's father came to Israel in 1949 at age 15. He worked in the market in Jerusalem, learning to cook from an old man who also came from Diyarbakir. He started Azura, his first restaurant, as a very simple establishment with four tables. The menu was Turkish with a Kurdish bent and included recipes from Elran's Persian mother. His father and mother both worked in the business and Elran has strong childhood memories of the sounds and smells of the kitchen. While Elran reminisces, we are served a delicious Kurdish kibbe with a herb and lemon sauce. It tastes like home; uncomplicated but superb ›home cooking‹. Elran's parents spoke Turkish and Farsi with each other, using Arabic in front of the children as their ›secret language‹. Like his father, Elran is at home with Arabic

»I learned from my father that good food has to be simple and authentic.«

culture and music, and his customers include both Arabs and Jews. He says, ›In reality it's the same culture.‹

Our host's trajectory in life and in the restaurant business was anything but linear. Elran, strong-willed and independent, considers himself to have been the problematic one of his siblings but the one most tied to the business. The army was not for him so he served time in jail instead. He eventually became responsible for the expansion of the Jerusalem Azura. A large restaurant next door to his father's, at the Machane Yehuda Market, opened when Elran was 18 years old. A couple of years later it closed. Elran felt it was time to expand the family business and took over the neighbouring restaurant with a handshake. ›What, do you want to be rich?‹ was his father's initial reaction. The restaurant was expanded to 50 tables and enjoyed great success. At the age of 22, Elran took over yet another Iraqi place at the market. There he served ›the food we ate ourselves‹, like Turkish dishes, Moroccan fish and *kneidlach* (matzah balls). This restaurant was a success as well, attracting guests from near and far. Elran had the necessary energy for a double life in the restaurant business, starting at 4 a.m. in his father's kitchen and then moving to his own in the late morning.

Nevertheless, Elran became bored: six years ago he left the family business and travelled around the world for three years. After returning to Israel he worked for a time at Arcadia, one of the best restaurants in Jerusalem, where he expanded his cooking techniques. Eventually, he moved to Ben Shemen near Tel Aviv, where he played shesh besh (backgammon) and felt increasingly depressed and isolated. One day, a friend happened upon an empty space in Tel Aviv and Elran's brothers convinced him to open his own restaurant there. This marked the birth of Azura Tel Aviv.

Elran designed ›his‹ Azura together with Eli Petel, head of the Bezalel Academy of Arts and Design in Jerusalem. It is beautifully done: simple and modern but with a warm atmosphere. On the first day it opened, there were lines to get in – certainly the result of the outstanding reputation of Azura in Jerusalem. Although Elran has made changes, family traditions are clearly evident, such as cooking on the small individual stoves. While he doesn't have a clear definition of what ›Israeli food‹ is, he knows exactly what his should be: ›I learned from my father that good food has to be simple and authentic.‹ His father, now 84, calls Elran the best cook in the family. When he comes to Tel Aviv to visit, he sits in the restaurant and smokes, visibly proud of his son. ›My father would never say it to me, but I can see it in his face!‹ Colourful, fragrant dishes are set in front of us: we taste the Kurdish- and Iraqi-style *kibbe*, *sofrito* and lamb that melts in the mouth. As Nuriel photographs the dishes, Elran's priorities are clear as he calls out: ›Hurry, before it gets cold!‹

LAMB SOFRITO WITH EGGPLANT & SPINACH

RECIPE FROM ELRAN SHREFLER

For 6 people as a main dish

- 1.5 kg (3 lb 5 oz) lamb neck (boneless, without fat)
- 4 tablespoons olive oil
- Sea salt
- Black pepper
- 6 potatoes
- 3 eggplant (aubergines)
- Canola oil, for deep-frying
- 500 g (1 lb 2 oz) baby spinach
- 2 onions
- 200 g (7 oz) lamb fat

Preheat the oven to 200°C (400°F). Cut the lamb meat into 3 cm (1¼ inch) cubes. Heat 2 tablespoons olive oil in an ovenproof saucepan, add the meat and brown on all sides. Season with salt and pepper and pour in 125 ml (4 fl oz) water. Cover the pan with foil or a lid and cook in the oven for about 2 hours.

Meanwhile, peel the potatoes and eggplant and cut into 1 cm (½ inch) cubes. Heat an ample amount of canola oil in a deep saucepan. Deep-fry the cubed vegetables a few at a time in the oil, drain on paper towels and set aside separately.

Cook the spinach slowly in a large saucepan with very little water until the liquid has evaporated. Set aside. Peel and quarter the onions. Heat 2 tablespoons olive oil in another frying pan, add the onions and sauté.

Place the lamb fat in a heavy-based saucepan and brown. Season the potatoes with salt and pepper and add to the pan. Layer half the onions and a third of the spinach and eggplant on top. Remove the meat from the oven and distribute evenly over the vegetables. Add the remaining onions, spinach and eggplant to the pan and season well. Pour in 250 ml (9 fl oz) water, cover the pan and simmer the stew over low heat for 1 hour, without stirring or adding any additional liquid.

Arrange sofrito on plates and serve hot.

HAYA'S TIP:
FRESH BREAD GOES WELL WITH SOFRITO. IT IS PERFECT FOR DIPPING IN THE DELICIOUS SAUCE.

KUBBEH HAMO

RECIPE FROM ELRAN SHREFLER

For 6 people as a main dish

For the soup:

- O 200 g (7 oz) dried chickpeas
- O 2 onions
- O 1 tablespoon olive oil
- O 1 tablespoon sea salt
- O 1½ teaspoons coarsely crushed black pepper
- O 1½ teaspoons ground turmeric
- O 1½ teaspoons hot curry powder
- O Pinch chilli flakes, plus extra to garnish

For the dough:

- O 300 g (10½ oz) fine bulgur
- O 1½ teaspoons sea salt
- O 150 g (5½ oz) semolina, plus extra for dusting
- O 100 g (3½ oz) minced chicken
- O Plain flour, for dusting

For the filling:

- O 3 tablespoons olive oil
- O 1 kg (2 lb 4 oz) minced beef (with fat, preferably from the neck)
- O 2 onions
- O 2 tomatoes
- O 1 teaspoon sea salt
- O 1 teaspoon black pepper
- O 1 teaspoon sweet paprika
- O Pinch chilli flakes

Put the chickpeas in a bowl, cover with water and soak overnight. The next day, strain and cook in a generous amount of fresh water until soft, about 1½ hours. Drain through a sieve.

While the chickpeas cook, prepare the kubbeh. For the *dough,* combine the bulgur and salt in a bowl. Add enough tepid water to cover the bulgur with 1 cm (½ inch) of water. Cover and leave to soak for 30 minutes.

Add the semolina and chicken to the bulgur and knead thoroughly with dampened hands until the mixture no longer sticks (you can also put it through a meat grinder). If the dough is too dry, add a bit more water; if it is too sticky, add a bit of flour. Cover with a tea towel and set aside.

For the *filling,* heat 2 tablespoons of olive oil in a pan, add the beef and cook until golden brown, 5–10 minutes. Then place in a sieve and drain the liquid.

Peel and finely dice the onions. Pour another 1 tablespoon of oil into the pan, add the onions and sauté. Coarsely cube the tomatoes. Mix together the drained meat, onions and tomatoes, and add the seasonings to taste.

On a work surface sprinkled with semolina, roll out the dough to a thickness of 3–5 mm (⅛–¼ inch). Sprinkle with semolina and cut out 12 circles about 10 cm (4 inches) in diameter. On half of the circles, place 1–2 tablespoons filling then cover with a second circle of dough. Carefully pull the edges of the dough around the filling and press firmly together to seal well. Keep the kubbeh and the remainder of the filling in the fridge until you are ready to cook them.

For the *soup,* peel and finely dice the onions. Heat the oil in a large saucepan, add the onions and sauté until golden brown. Add the spices and briefly sauté. Add the cooked chickpeas, pour in 1.5 litres (52 fl oz) water and bring to the boil. Carefully lay the kubbeh in the soup, add the rest of the meat filling and simmer for 20 minutes in the soup.

Arrange soup and kubbeh in deep plates and sprinkle with chilli flakes.

SSANGYONG
NOFF

THE SURVIVOR

MATI LANDSTEIN

Mati Matalon 41
»The Survivor«

Mati Landstein's little corner bar in the Levinsky Market is a fixture of the neighbourhood, serving cold beer from the tap, chopped liver, pickles, sardines and horseradish.

It is late morning when we meet Mati. At nearly 90 years of age, Mati moves slowly but is still mentally sharp and full of humour. He's wearing a baseball cap and a faded T-shirt emblazoned with a large Smirnoff vodka bottle. Like so many of his generation in Israel, Mati is a Holocaust survivor with a tragic but also life-affirming story. He sits with us at one of the small sidewalk tables and looks very much at home. It is quite obvious that we are not the first people who have been granted an audience with him. He speaks slowly in Hebrew and interrupts his story only to pat a passing dog or to return the friendly greetings from passers-by. He is hugged again and again, and we sense how beloved he is, that he is seen as a sort of hero in this neighbourhood. The longer Mati talks, the more apparent it is to us that we are face to face with a survivor in the truest sense of the word.

His odyssey began in Warsaw. Mati was born in 1929; he was to lose his entire family in the war. Confined to the Warsaw Ghetto, both parents died of typhus at the end of 1942. From then on, Mati and his two brothers lived alone and were not allowed to leave the apartment after 8 p.m. One day his older brother ignored the curfew and was shot dead. His younger brother tried to escape to Russia, but Mati never heard from him again. At the age of 16 he was alone. He and a number of other Jews eventually escaped from the ghetto through an underground tunnel. During their flight, grenades were thrown into the sewers and Mati lost an eye in the process.

In 1947 he made it to Lodz by himself and then took the train to Verbier, Switzerland, where he waited five months until he finally found transport to Israel. He can still recall the name of the boat: Nachshon Hakastel. But the journey was not without its problems. Because the British were stopping and redirecting all boats heading for Israel, Mati was stranded in Cyprus for four months. At some point he obtained a fake I.D. to make himself four years younger; only those under 18 and over 55 years of age were being allowed into Israel.

Mati eventually made Aliyah (the immigration of Jews to Israel). He travelled from Haifa to Kibbutz Glil Yam, joined the army in 1950 and did a two-year service. But instead of returning to the kibbutz, he moved with eight like-minded people into a house in Jaffa that, as he freely admits, had been taken over from fleeing Arabs.

In 1953 he decided to return to France on his Israeli passport. He had heard that, as a refugee, he was entitled to money from the German government, so he secretly made his way across the border from France to Germany. He was captured, however, and spent 21 days in jail for crossing the border illegally. When he was released, he received money from the German government and was informed that he could emigrate to Brazil, Argentina or Uruguay.

Mati decided on Brazil, although he had been warned that ›it's a jungle there‹. His reply to this was always: ›No jungle can break me!‹ Arriving in the harbour of Santos, 30 days after departing from Genoa, he recalls that he didn't know what to look at first – Brazil was more modern than Europe at that time! When he got his entry papers, he went on to Rio and spent the next 21 years in Brazil.

»Life is good! No complaints!«

›Brazil is huge, endless,‹ he says. He built a life for himself, married a Jewish woman with Polish/ Romanian roots in Rio and moved with her to Sao Paolo. They had three children – one son and two daughters – who all attended a Hebrew school, and with whom he spoke Portuguese at home.

Mati ran an import/export business in Brazil and quickly became rich. So when he moved to Israel with his family he had plenty of money. The first things he bought with it were an apartment and a car – a home and a means for exploring the surrounding area were especially important for him at that time.

At this point in our conversation, Mati orders his third vodka, and it is not yet noon. The man who brings it to him kisses him on the cheek and, with great affection, calls him abba (father). Mati has done a great deal for the neighbourhood and for the people who live here, and they respect him for his character. He says, ›I cannot stand racism or aggression against immigrants,‹ adding: ›Hunger and sickness are the two worst things in the world.‹

In 1974 Mati bought this bar, which had been serving draught beer since 1935. He continued the tradition and added small meat dishes and gambas to go with the beer. At the beginning he arrived at work every day at 5 a.m., and most of his customers were hardworking people who came here for a beer and simple food. Not much has changed since then. Mati's place is still known for its particularly good beer, thanks to a wonderful old cooling system that ensures that the beer comes out of the tap at just the right temperature.

Now Mati's grandson Shmulik is here every day from 9 a.m. to 4:30 pm, and then Mati's son Itzchak comes in the evening and stays until closing time. Mati declares, ›Baruch Hashem ("Thank God" or "God Willing"), I will continue to be here every day.‹ He also tells us that, because he prefers drinking vodka, he will only drink beer if a customer complains about it, in which case he has to taste it. Once again, Mati exclaims, ›Baruch Hashem!‹ as he explains, ›I worked in the bar for 21 years. I'm 89 now and have nothing to complain about. At home I have eight grandchildren and an 81-year-old wife waiting for me.‹ We share Mati's happiness about his old age and his brood of grandchildren and are deeply moved when he bids us farewell by saying: ›Life is good! No complaints!‹

DUCK CONFIT WITH JERUSALEM ARTICHOKES

For 4 people as a main dish

For the sauce:
- O 500 g (1 lb 2 oz) oxtail
- O 5 French shallots
- O 500 ml (17 fl oz) red wine
- O 200 ml (7 fl oz) port
- O 1 bay leaf
- O 5 black peppercorns
- O 1 star anise
- O 50 g (1¾ oz) butter
- O Sea salt

HAYA'S TIP: THE LONG COOKING TIME OF THE OXTAIL CAN BE REDUCED TO 1½ HOURS WITH THE USE OF A PRESSURE COOKER.

For the duck confit:
- O 4 duck legs
- O 1 tablespoon sea salt
- O 1–2 litres (35–70 fl oz) canola oil

For the Jerusalem artichokes:
- O 500 g (1 lb 2 oz) Jerusalem artichokes
- O ½ teaspoon sea salt
- O 300 ml (10½ fl oz) cream

- O 4 egg yolks (at room temperature)
- O Sea salt
- O 4 sprigs dill

For the *sauce*, preheat the oven to 220°C (425°F). Roast the oxtail on a baking tray or in an ovenproof dish in the oven for 10–15 minutes.

Place the meat, including the bones, in a large saucepan. Halve the unpeeled shallots and add to the pan with the wine, port and 5 litres (170 fl oz) of water. Bring to the boil and simmer for 6 hours. (If the pan cannot fit all of the water, pour in as much as possible at the beginning and gradually add the rest later. The meat should always be covered with liquid.)

After about 3 hours, begin preparing the *duck*. Salt the legs and place them tightly together – but not on top of each other – in a wide pan. Pour the oil over the top to completely cover the meat. Cook the duck over low heat until the meat is so soft that you can pierce it with a spoon, about 3 hours.

About 1 hour before the oxtail is to finish cooking, prepare the *Jerusalem artichokes*. Preheat the oven to 250°C (500°F). Peel the tubers and artichokes in an ovenproof dish. Season with salt and pour the cream over the top. Cover with foil and bake in the oven until soft, about 70 minutes.

Strain the oxtail, catching the liquid and returning it to the pan. Add the spices and boil to reduce the liquid to 200 ml (7 fl oz). Stir the butter into the sauce and salt to taste.

Remove the artichokes from the oven. Reduce oven to 240°C (475°F). Carefully lift the duck legs out of the hot oil, place in an ovenproof dish and roast for 5–10 minutes in the oven.

Pull the oxtail meat off the bones and arrange on plates with the artichokes and duck. Pour the sauce over the duck and place one raw egg yolk on each serving of meat. Lightly salt the egg, garnish with dill and serve.

SWEETS

FRUIT, ICE CREAM, BISCUITS AND CAKES

Caramelised pineapple is a classic NENI dessert. This variant is a kind of edible piña colada: paper-thin slices of the sweet pineapple are combined with coconut ice cream, with a few drops of fresh, fruity olive oil acting as a ›flavour bridge‹ between the two. And the chilli threads give the dish a special kick.

PINEAPPLE CARPACCIO WITH COCONUT ICE CREAM

For 6 people as a dessert

For the pineapple carpaccio:

- 1 large untreated pineapple, about 1.3 kg / 3 lb after it has been peeled
- 150 g (5½ oz) sugar
- 50 ml (1½ fl oz) rum
- Grated zest of 1 untreated lime
- Grated zest of 1 untreated orange
- 1 tablespoon natural vanilla extract, or use the seeds of 1 vanilla bean, mixed with 1 tablespoon rum
- 30 ml (1 fl oz) lime juice

For the ice cream:

- 100 ml (3½ fl oz) milk
- 35 g (1¼ oz) shredded coconut
- 260 ml (9 fl oz) coconut milk
- 70 g (2½ oz) sugar
- 2 egg yolks

- Chilli threads
- Olive oil

For the *carpaccio,* preheat the oven to 180°C (350°F). Peel the pineapple, reserving the peel. Cut out the black eyes of the peeled pineapple in a spiral fashion so that when you have finished the surface of the peeled fruit looks similar to a screw.

Place the pineapple peel in a saucepan, bring to the boil with 50 g (1¾ oz) sugar, the rum and 1.5 litres (52 fl oz) of water and simmer for about 15 minutes. Strain and keep the sauce.

Mix 100 g (3½ oz) sugar with the citrus zest and spread out on a large plate. Brush the pineapple with the vanilla extract, then roll in the sugar–zest mixture so that the fruit is well coated on all sides. (Those who like it really sweet can stir the remaining sugar into the sauce.)

Place the pineapple upright in an ovenproof saucepan and pour the strained sauce over the top. Bake for 1½–2 hours in the oven, basting with the liquid every 10–15 minutes so that it caramelises. (If the liquid evaporates, heat a bit of water with sugar to pour over the pineapple.) Remove from the oven, leave to cool and cut into paper-thin slices. Save any juices and mix with the lime juice.

While the pineapple is in the oven, begin the *ice cream*. Bring the milk to the boil in a saucepan with the shredded coconut, remove from the heat and leave for 30 minutes. Then purée in a blender for 3 minutes to make a smooth liquid and set aside.

In a medium-sized saucepan, heat the coconut milk along with 35 g (1¼ oz) sugar to 75°C (165°F) – check with a kitchen thermometer. Beat the remaining sugar with the egg yolks until foamy.

Add the egg yolk mixture to the coconut milk and whisk constantly over very low heat until thick and creamy. Take care that the temperature does not exceed 80°C (175°F) or you might get scrambled egg. The cream is ready if you can make a wavy pattern in it by blowing on a small amount of cream on the back of a wooden spoon – in cooking jargon this is called ›blowing a rose‹.

Stir the puréed coconut into the still-warm egg mixture until the two components are well blended, then pass through a fine-meshed sieve and churn in an ice cream maker.

Arrange the pineapple slices on plates and drizzle with the pineapple-lime juice. Place one scoop of coconut ice cream on each plate and garnish with the chilli threads and a few drops of olive oil.

HAYA'S TIPS:
THE INDIVIDUAL COMPONENTS OF THIS DISH CAN BE MADE A DAY IN ADVANCE.

THIS RECIPE PRODUCES MORE ICE CREAM THAN NEEDED FOR THIS DESSERT, BUT IT IS DIFFICULT TO MAKE A SMALLER AMOUNT.

KEEP THE LEFT-OVER ICE CREAM IN THE FREEZER FOR ANOTHER TIME. TAKE IT OUT 10 MINUTES BEFORE YOU ARE READY TO SERVE – THIS WILL RESTORE ITS CREAMY CONSISTENCY.

Dates and honey are frequently served on Rosh Hashanah, the Jewish New Year. They are a symbol for the coming year: people wish each other that it will be just as sweet as the fruit.

DATE CAKE WITH SALTY CARAMEL SAUCE

For 4–6 people as a dessert

For the batter:
- O 250 g (9 oz) medjool dates
- O 1 teaspoon baking powder
- O 50 g (1¾ oz) walnuts
- O 50 g (1¾ oz) pecans
- O 60 g (2¼ oz) soft butter (at room temperature), plus extra for greasing
- O 200 g (7 oz) muscovado sugar
- O 3 eggs
- O 125 g (4½ oz) puffed amaranth
- O 75 g (2½ oz) ground almonds
- O ½ teaspoon ground cinnamon
- O ½ teaspoon ground ginger
- O ½ teaspoon sea salt

For the caramel sauce:
- O 300 g (10½ oz) muscovado sugar
- O 230 ml (8 fl oz) cream
- O 150 g (5½ oz) butter
- O 1 tablespoon lemon juice
- O ½ teaspoon natural vanilla extract, or the seeds of 1 vanilla bean
- O ½ teaspoon sea salt

- O Icing sugar, for dusting

For the *batter,* pit and coarsely chop the dates. Place in a saucepan with 480 ml (16¼ fl oz) water, slowly bring to the boil and simmer until the dates are soft, about 10 minutes. Remove from the heat, stir in the baking powder and leave to cool.

Preheat the oven to 200°C (400°F). Lightly dry-roast the walnuts and pecans in a frying pan and coarsely chop. Beat the butter and sugar with a mixer until fluffy. Add the eggs and continue to beat until airy. Add the dates and the remaining ingredients and beat for 1 more minute.

Lightly butter a 22 cm (8½ inch) roasting tin or ovenproof dish. Pour the batter into the tin or dish and bake in the oven for 50–60 minutes.

While the cake bakes, slowly bring all ingredients for the *caramel sauce* to the boil in a small saucepan. Simmer until the liquid thickens, about 10 minutes.

When the date cake is cooked, cut into individual portions, arrange on plates, drizzle with warm caramel sauce and dust with icing sugar.

HAYA'S TIPS:
I LIKE TO BAKE THE CAKE IN INDIVIDUAL PORTIONS IN SMALL MOULDS; THE BAKING TIME IS THEN REDUCED TO 20–30 MINUTES.

THE TOASTED PECANS CAN BE REPLACED WITH CARAMELISED PECANS (PAGE 261).

PRICKLY PEAR–MANGO SALAD WITH PRICKLY PEAR SORBET

For 4 people as a dessert

For the salad:
- 300 g (10½ oz) mangoes (chilled)
- 300 g (10½ oz) prickly pears (chilled)
- 1 tablespoon lime juice
- Grated zest of 1 untreated lime
- 2 tablespoons honey

For the sorbet:
- 250 g (9 oz) peaches
- 250 g (9 oz) sugar
- 700 g (1 lb 9 oz) prickly pears
- 80 ml (2½ fl oz) lime juice

- Mint leaves, to garnish

HAYA'S TIPS:
A BIT LESS SORBET IS NEEDED FOR THIS DESSERT THAN THE RECIPE MAKES, BUT IT IS DIFFICULT TO MAKE A SMALLER AMOUNT IN AN ICE CREAM MAKER. IF YOU WOULD LIKE TO TRY ANYWAY, YOU CAN HALVE THE AMOUNTS GIVEN. BUT USUALLY NOTHING IS LEFT OVER EVEN IF YOU MAKE A FULL RECIPE. AND IF IT IS, PUT IT IN THE FREEZER, AND YOU ARE READY FOR THE NEXT SURPRISE GUESTS.

THE SALAD SHOULD BE VERY COLD WHEN SERVED, SO RETURN IT TO THE REFRIGERATOR AFTER YOU HAVE PREPARED IT AND LET IT CHILL.

For the *salad,* peel the mangoes and prickly pears. Remove the mango seed and cut the fruit into about 5 cm (2 inch) pieces (they don't have to be the exact same size – that makes the salad more exciting). Blend the lime juice, lime zest and honey together in a bowl and fold in the fruit. Chill in the refrigerator until you are ready to serve it.

For the *sorbet,* stone the peaches and cut into about 2 cm (¾ inch) cubes. Mix together with the sugar in a saucepan and cook over high heat, stirring constantly, until the sugar has completely dissolved. Leave to cool.

Peel the prickly pears and briefly purée with a blender. Pass through a sieve to remove the seeds.

Weigh out 250 g (9 oz) of prickly pear purée and blend with the peaches and lime juice until smooth, then churn in an ice cream maker.

Arrange the sorbet and salad on plates and garnish with mint leaves.

Prickly pear, called *sabra* in Hebrew, is sold at street stands in Israel. The fruit lies in large wooden boxes filled with ice cubes. Elihay and his friends once tried their luck as prickly pear hawkers. They picked the prickly fruits with the sharpened edge of an aluminium can. To avoid getting hurt, they rubbed off the prickles with sand and then washed the sabras very thoroughly. They never earned much money from their sales, however, because they ate most of their wares themselves.

The prickly pear is also a symbol for Israelis. It is said that they, like the fruit, are prickly on the outside and soft on the inside. It is the Israeli version of ›hard shell, soft core‹.

Dallal
Aner Zalel

THE PHILOSOPHER

ANER ZALEL

Dallal Bakery
»The Philosopher«

»If you made a bagel from croissant dough, would you still call it a bagel?«

Dallal Bakery, located in a flower-filled side street in the trendy Neve Tzedek neighbourhood, is already full at mid-morning. All outside tables are taken, even the ones added to a small park-like area directly across the street. We sit outside in the French wicker chairs at the long marble counter. Inside the bakery, customers crowd around the large glass cases in which croissants, walnut pastries, cinnamon rolls, fruit bars and other delicacies are stacked. The shop's sales counters are laden with freshly baked bread, bagels, and an assortment of cakes. Much here is clearly inspired by the bars and cafés of France – this is also a part of Tel Aviv.

We are here to meet Aner, the head of Dallal Bakery – a baker-cum-philosopher. His utmost dedication to his work and whimsical sense of humour permeate our conversation. ›I love this »primitive« job,‹ he says, ›because you have to be fully involved in what you're doing. Computers are not essential here.‹ He likes to joke with his employees and can be simultaneously strict and friendly. He good-naturedly teases a young American waitress, a dancer working here as a side job – navigating this busy place with very little Hebrew – as he asks her to bring us an assortment of baked goods to taste. We observe not for the first time that one does not necessarily have to speak Hebrew to get along in Tel Aviv.

Aner launches into baking details: he puts more butter into the croissants than the French do, ›because I like it‹. He brings us an exquisite puff pastry with caramelised apples, and then sweet bagels sprinkled with sesame seeds, ›like in Jerusalem‹. He traces the outlines of one of the croissants, explaining: ›As soon as you change the shape, you change the baking time and the taste as well.‹ We learn that in the cool temperatures of winter, the dough behaves very differently than it does now, in late summer. Aner's croissants are crisp on the outside but chewy and fluffy inside. We eagerly take a bite but then he stops us: ›You have to smell them first! Like a good wine.‹

Dallal is where ›baked nostalgia‹, as Aner calls it, is created. His grandmother had run away from Belarus, where she had been a baker. In Israel in the early 1930s she met his communist grandfather from Russia, a building engineer. Both grandparents helped set up Kibbutz Eilon, in western Galilee. The socialist-oriented kibbutzim, with all decisions made jointly by the community, played a much more important role in the early history of the Jewish settlement than they do today. Kibbutz Eilon already had a German baker, so Aner's grandmother was put to work making sweaters. Aner, who lived in the kibbutz children's house until he was eight, can still recall the stacks of his grandma's

Burda magazines with their knitting patterns. The family eventually moved to Haifa but returned to the kibbutz often for visits. ›Life on the kibbutz made me strong,‹ he recalls.

As a teenager, Aner often accompanied his father – also an engineer – on irrigation projects to many African countries. Like most Israelis, he also served in the army as a young man. His grandmother, still a passionate baker, often sent him care packages there: coconut chocolate or cinnamon chocolate. On those occasions, Aner was especially popular with his unit. Also like most Israelis, Aner travelled around the world post-army. With a sly smile, Aner recounts meeting Katie, who would become his wife and mother of his children, when he replaced Katie as a cook on a cattle station in the north of Australia. She was from the U.K. and had trained him for a week and then left. She stayed in his mind, however, so he decided to go find her, and after many attempts, finally ran into her in a bar full of British expats watching Princess Diana's funeral! Aner went with Katie to London, where he trained at Le Cordon Bleu and volunteered as an unpaid apprentice at the Ritz. In 1999, the couple lived for a time in Israel, where Aner started working at Arcadia in Jerusalem, but they returned to England. Aner worked at Ottolenghi and met Patrick Lozach, from whom he learned more about making French pastries and breads.

When Aner took over the bakery at Dallal in Tel Aviv in 2008, he began to create what he calls, ›Israeli nostalgia‹ – linking Ashkenazi baking to traditional French pastry making. The baking artistry of his grandmother had introduced him to the traditional breads and cakes of the Ashkenazi Jews from Poland, Belarus and all of Eastern Europe. He taught his bakers to make *rugelach*, feather-light dough rolls filled with jam and nuts. While we sample his *rugelach*, Aner muses about tradition, but he also welcomes change: while his grandmother used margarine for her baked goods, he uses butter – loads of it!

›What does it take to be a good baker?‹ we ask him. His answer is

at once simple and complicated: principles and intellectual curiosity, which apply to everything from what goes into making a croissant to how to best live one's life. Aner also places the utmost importance on quality and details. He has the reputation of constantly ›nagging and feeling the dough‹. Aner takes us into the bakery and shows us his ingredients. He gets his flour from all over Europe: for pastries from Italy and for bread from Germany. He especially likes the rough texture of Germany's rye flour, for example. By now it has become abundantly clear that he is incredibly fascinated by flour and dough and their idiosyncrasies.

Aner sees himself as a craftsman, not as an artist. The philosopher emerges: ›No chef can ever invent anything completely new. Just like the chair maker in Herman Hesse's *Narcissus and Goldmund*, whose furniture can change a bit, but a chair still remains a chair!‹ Nevertheless, he strives to constantly develop his baking artistry and is always improving on details. His brioche, for example, is made with no fewer than three different kinds of dough, because for him that is the only way to do it. ›We are creatures of comfort,‹ he smiles, and cheerfully adds: ›We live to eat!‹

Aner's children want to become bakers, like their father and grandmother. But Aner is hesitant: ›First they should go to university,‹ he says. Small bakeries in Tel Aviv, like everywhere else, have a hard time surviving in the shadow of the big chains. The lifestyle and hours of a baker are also unappealing for many young people. Nevertheless, business is good at Dallal. They have a staff of 16 and always draw a large crowd, both locals and tourists. Aner also recalls when he started out and was working six days a week and sometimes even taking his 18-month-old baby with him to the bakery. He now works only five days a week and has more time for his family. We ask him who cooks at home. He laughs: ›The kitchen is the only place where my wife and I fight.‹ He then adds, ›Cooking is easy; baking is a much bigger challenge.‹ We are sure that his grandmother would agree.

MA'AMOUL COOKIES

RECIPE FROM ANER ZALEL

For 30–40 cookies

For the dough:

- O 320 g (11 oz) plain flour, plus extra for dusting
- O 4 tablespoons almond meal
- O 120 g (4¼ oz) icing sugar
- O 200 g (7 oz) cold butter
- O 1 large egg

For the filling:

- O 20 g (¾ oz) walnuts
- O 20 g (¾ oz) unsalted pistachios
- O 40 g (1½ oz) sugar
- O ½ teaspoon ground cinnamon
- O Pinch freshly ground nutmeg
- O Pinch ground ginger
- O Pinch ground cardamom
- O 60 g (2¼ oz) date paste

- O Icing sugar, for dusting

For the *dough*, mix the dry ingredients with the flat beater attachment of your mixer. Dice the butter, add to the bowl and continue beating until it has a sandy consistency. Add the egg and keep beating to make a smooth dough.

Knead the dough for a few minutes by hand, wrap in plastic and chill in the fridge for at least 1 hour or overnight.

On a floured work surface, roll out the dough to a thickness of 2 mm (1⁄16 inch) and cut into 2 equal rectangles. Lay the dough pieces on baking paper and chill for 30 more minutes.

Meanwhile, for the *filling*, coarsely chop all the ingredients except the date paste in a food processor. Gently warm the date paste in a small saucepan with 3 tablespoons water until it melts.

Preheat the oven to 190°C (375°F). Spread half the date paste thinly on each of the dough sheets and sprinkle each with half the nut-spice mixture. Roll up the dough with the filling from the long side and score the top diagonally at 1 cm (½ inch) intervals.

Bake the dough rolls in the oven until light brown, about 20 minutes. Remove and leave to cool a little. Cut into 1 cm (½ inch) slices at the incisions and dust with icing sugar.

CHALLA

RECIPE FROM ANER ZALEL

For 2 challas

- O 460 g (1 lb) plain flour plus extra for dusting
- O 45 g (1½ oz) sugar
- O 7 g (¼ oz) salt
- O 9 g (¼ oz) dried yeast
- O 30 g (1 oz) butter (at room temperature)
- O 2 large eggs
- O 230 ml (8 fl oz) water
- O Sesame seeds, for sprinkling

HAYA'S TIP:
I LIKE CHALLA BEST WITH A SWEET GLAZE. I SIMPLY STIR TOGETHER A BIT OF EGG WHITE WITH DATE OR MAPLE SYRUP AND BRUSH THE CHALLA WITH THIS MIXTURE.

Beat the flour, sugar, salt and yeast using the flat beater attachment of your mixer. Dice butter and stir in well.

Add 1 egg and the water and process with the dough hook until the dough is smooth and elastic. Cover with a damp cloth or plastic wrap and leave to rise for 45 minutes at room temperature.

Divide the dough into 6 pieces of equal size. On a floured surface, shape each piece into a ball, then roll into a rope about 20 cm (8 inches) long.

Braid 3 ropes at a time together into a plait. Carefully place on a baking tray lined with baking paper, cover and leave to rise at room temperature until the plaits have doubled in size, about 1 hour.

Preheat the oven to 200°C (400°F). Beat the second egg with 2 tablespoons water and brush the challas with it, then sprinkle with sesame seeds.

Place an ovenproof pan of hot water in the bottom of the oven and bake the challas for 10 minutes. Remove the pan of water and bake the challas for another 10–20 minutes, until golden brown. Leave to cool on a wire rack.

KNAFEH TATIN WITH PLUMS

Makes a 28 cm (11 inch) tart

- 700 g (1 lb 9 oz) plums
- 200 g (7 oz) sugar
- 130 g (4½ oz) butter, plus extra for greasing
- 120 ml (3¾ fl oz) cream
- 1 tablespoon lemon juice
- 1 pinch sea salt
- 200 g (7 oz) kataifi pastry (angel hair)
- Icing sugar, for dusting

Preheat the oven to 220°C (425°F). Halve and stone the plums. Caramelise the sugar in a wide saucepan, add 55 g (2 oz) butter and stir until melted. Add the cream and 50 ml (1½ fl oz) water and slowly bring to the boil, stirring to dissolve the sugar. Boil down for several minutes to make a creamy sauce, then stir in the lemon juice and salt. Add the plums and toss in the sauce.

Melt 75 g (2½ oz) butter in a small saucepan. On a work surface or in a bowl, pull apart the kataifi pastry strings a bit with your hands, pour the butter over the top and briefly stir. (This makes the dough strings softer and easier to work with.)

Butter the tart pan. Spoon in the plums with the sauce and cover with the kataifi pastry strings. Bake in the oven until golden brown, about 10 minutes. Then take out and unmould onto a large plate (taking care not to burn yourself, as the hot juice of the fruit can leak out). Dust with icing sugar and serve warm.

HAYA'S TIP:
A DELICIOUS COMPLEMENT TO THIS DISH IS HOMEMADE YOGHURT ICE CREAM. IT IS EASY TO MAKE AS IT CONSISTS OF ONLY 3 INGREDIENTS. FOR ABOUT 640 ML (22 FL OZ) OF ICE CREAM YOU NEED 500 G (1 LB 2 OZ) OF GREEK YOGHURT, 100 G (3½ OZ) OF SUGAR AND 2 TABLESPOONS OF LIME JUICE. THOROUGHLY STIR ALL INGREDIENTS TOGETHER AND CHURN IN AN ICE CREAM MAKER. READY TO EAT!

ORANGE FRENCH TOAST WITH ALMOND CREAM

For 4–6 people as a breakfast or to serve with coffee

For the orange syrup:
- 60 ml (2 fl oz) water
- 60 g (2¼ oz) sugar
- Grated zest of 1 untreated orange
- 2 tablespoons Grand Marnier

For the almond cream:
- 200 g (7 oz) flaked almonds
- 100 g (3½ oz) icing sugar
- Pinch salt
- 2 large eggs
- 100 g (3½ oz) butter (at room temperature)
- 1 tablespoon brandy
- 1–2 drops bitter almond extract (optional)

- 4–6 slices challa (page 253)
- 50 g (1¾ oz) flaked almonds
- Icing sugar, for dusting

For the *orange syrup,* bring all the ingredients except the Grand Marnier to the boil in a small saucepan and simmer for about 5 minutes, stirring to dissolve the sugar. Remove from the heat, add the Grand Marnier and let the syrup cool to room temperature.

For the *almond cream,* finely grind the flaked almonds in a food processor along with the sugar and salt. Add the eggs, butter, brandy and bitter almond extract and blend until creamy.

Preheat the oven to 200°C (400°F). Lay the challa slices on a baking tray lined with baking paper, brush both sides with the syrup and spread the top with almond cream. Sprinkle with flaked almonds and bake until the tops are golden brown, about 15 minutes. Remove from the oven and dust with icing sugar. Serve warm.

HAYA'S TIPS:
LEFT-OVER ALMOND CREAM WILL KEEP IN THE REFRIGERATOR FOR UP TO 1 WEEK.

FOR CHILDREN, THE GRAND MARNIER CAN SIMPLY BE REPLACED WITH THE SAME AMOUNT OF ORANGE JUICE, AND THE BRANDY CAN BE LEFT OUT ENTIRELY.

FOR A DELICIOUS ALTERNATIVE TO CHALLA, TRY HALVED, SLIGHTLY STALE CROISSANTS.

SESAME³

For 4 people as a dessert

For the muscovado ice cream:

- O 500 ml (17 fl oz) coconut milk
- O 100 g (3½ oz) muscovado sugar
- O 50 g (1¾ oz) Japanese short-grain rice

- O 40 g (1½ oz) sesame seeds
- O Plain tahini, for drizzling
- O Date syrup, for drizzling
- O 40 g (1½ oz) halva
- O 50 g (1¾ oz) caramelised pecans (page 261)

HAYA'S TIPS:
IF YOU DON'T HAVE AN ICE CREAM MAKER, YOU CAN POUR THE ICE CREAM MIXTURE INTO A FREEZER-PROOF CONTAINER AND FREEZE IT. GIVE IT A GOOD STIR EVERY 30 MINUTES OR SO WITH A FORK. THE CONSISTENCY IS THEN SIMILAR TO THAT OF THE ITALIAN *GRANITA*. THE AMOUNTS CALLED FOR ARE ENOUGH FOR MORE THAN 4 PORTIONS, BUT THE MIXTURE IS SIMPLY EASIER TO WORK WITH THIS WAY – AND YOU ALSO HAVE ICE CREAM ON HAND TO SNACK ON. IF YOU DON'T WANT TO HAVE ANY LEFT OVER, HALVE THE AMOUNTS GIVEN OR JUST EAT IT ALL UP.

IT'S BEST TO USE STRING HALVA; THIS IS OFTEN AVAILABLE AT KOSHER FOOD SHOPS OR ISRAELI GROCERS. IF YOU ARE ONLY ABLE TO FIND WHOLE HALVA, CRUMBLE IT BETWEEN YOUR FINGERS TO MAKE THIS DESSERT.

For the *ice cream*, bring the coconut milk, muscovado sugar and rice to the boil in a saucepan. Cover and simmer until very soft, about 45 minutes. Stir occasionally so it doesn't stick.

Blitz the rice mixture with a blender to make a smooth paste and pass through a sieve. Pour into an ice cream maker and process until creamy.

Dry-roast sesame seeds in a small frying pan over medium heat until golden brown; leave to cool.

Scatter the roasted sesame seeds on serving plates. Place 1 scoop of ice cream on each plate and drizzle with tahini and date syrup. Add halva and pecans and serve immediately.

This dish is the result of a search for a vegan dessert for the restaurants of the 25Hours Hotels chain. We experimented a great deal during this time to create an ice cream with an especially creamy consistency – long-cooked rice was the solution.

CARAMELISED PECANS

For 250 g (9 oz)

- O 1 cardamom pod
- O 250 g (9 oz) sugar
- O 1 cinnamon stick
- O 1 star anise
- O 250 g (9 oz) pecans
- O Canola oil, for deep-frying

Coarsely grind the cardamom pod in a mortar, then bring to the boil in a saucepan with the sugar, cinnamon stick, anise and 625 ml (21½ fl oz) water. Add the pecans and simmer for 45 minutes, stirring occasionally and keeping the nuts covered with water.

Strain the nuts and drain in a sieve.

In a deep saucepan, heat a generous amount of canola oil to 180°C (360°F) on a kitchen thermometer and deep-fry the nuts a few at a time until brown but not burned, 2–3 minutes.

Remove the nuts from the oil with a mesh skimmer, place on a baking tray (without baking paper) and allow to cool completely.

HAYA'S TIPS:
THE NUTS WILL CONTINUE TO DARKEN EVEN AFTER FRYING, SO TAKE THEM OUT WHEN THEY ARE A BIT LIGHTER THAN IN THE PICTURE. STORED IN AN AIRTIGHT CONTAINER, THEY WILL KEEP FOR 3–4 WEEKS.

THE NUTS ARE ALSO GOOD WITH DATE PUDDING (PAGE 241), BUT I LIKE TO NIBBLE THEM PLAIN.

THE ALCHEMIST

BENNY BRIGA

Café Levinsky 41

»The Alchemist«

With a mischievous smile and bundles of energy, Benny greets us and immediately sets to work concocting an assortment of his specialty natural flavour sodas, for which he is well known in the Levinsky Market and beyond. He is an alchemist with a flowing mane of hair, working from his small, beautifully designed street stand – a kiosk lined with glass shelves to hold the rows of large jars filled with preserved plants, herbs, chilli peppers, flowers and fermented fruit. They contain the essence for his colourful drinks, the secrets of their special flavours. Benny is a cheerful fixture in the neighbourhood. In front of his stand is parked a small open truck that has been converted into a miniature pub garden. On the covered cargo area are two simple benches offering a shady place to sit and rest on this busy street. The roof of the truck's cab is decorated with flowerpots and herbs; we see plants and wildflowers everywhere, signalling the inspiration for Benny's drinks and setting the tone for nature's part in his creations.

Benny started his business five years ago selling good coffee from vintage espresso machines, as well as liqueurs and jams. Soon customers began asking for *gazoz*, flavoured soda water with a long tradition in Tel Aviv. So Benny started experimenting with flowers, leaves and herbs, discovered fermentation, read up on the uses of kefir – fermented milk – and began creating one flavour after another. One day his friend Inbal, who runs a tourism company called Delicious Israel, and who had also encouraged him to include *gazoz* in his offerings, brought Chicago mayor Rahm Emanuel to visit his stand. His new beverages were a hit with his famous customer as well, and Benny never looked back. Today his all-natural *gazoz* is the heart of his business.

While Benny tells us this, he is putting a variety of herbs and leaves in several jars on the counter. Fresh berries and a few blossoms go in as well, and each jar emits a different aroma. We observe Benny in his process of creation. There is a special rule here: one does not order a drink; Benny chats with each of his customers and then creates a unique mixture that he feels is right for that person. We're served our personal drinks. The unanimous conclusion: delicious, for each of us.

For the past year, the *gazoz* sorcerer has been interested in the fermentation processes mastered by the Koreans and Japanese. ›Fermentation is always a process of long experimentation – it is a matter of trial and error,‹ he says. He constantly wants to learn more and reads incessantly about the subject. He tells us about a book called *The Art of Fermentation*, which Benny refers to as the ›bible‹ of fermentation and from which he draws many of his ideas. The more he learns, the more Benny's interest in botany and the use of natural foods grows. It does not surprise us that Heela Harel (page 82), our urban forager, provides him with many of his ingredients.

Benny cites the important health and medical properties in all of this as well, recounting how his grandmother often cured him with herbs. His grandparents fermented ginger, radishes and horseradish. Benny holds up a yellow ghost chilli that he also ferments, along with many other herbs and spices, to illustrate that a great variety of natural ingredients can be used to make his drinks. The alchemist is in his element.

Benny was born in 1975 in Or Yehuda, near Tel Aviv. When he, his brother and two sisters grew up there it was like a small village surrounded by nature; in the years since then, it has grown into a city.

»Fermentation is a matter of trial and error.«

Benny has strong childhood memories of both music and food. His father, who was born in Libya and whose family lived there for over 400 years, loves music and sang Arabic songs all day long. His mother, whose family is from Istanbul, and his Libyan grandparents cooked at home, with every meal featuring four or five different dishes.

As Benny recounts his past, a picture of a man of contradictions and surprises emerges. At the age of 14, he left home to attend a military boarding school in Haifa. Benny smiles when he thinks back to this time. Despite incurring the first of many serious injuries in his life while at boarding school, those years are still among his favourite memories. He spent a great deal of time outdoors and met the person who remains his best friend today. He eventually left Haifa and returned home to finish high school and then focused his studies on film and politics.

After the army, where he was again injured, Benny travelled in South America for a year and caught the ›cooking virus‹ in Brazil. He returned to Tel Aviv, which he describes as ›a city that for me is like the world, full of young people coming and going and changing‹. He took all kinds of odd jobs and by his own account led a very unstable life. Similar to his herbs, Benny appears both sweet and tough! After a bad motorbike accident on Levinsky Street, resulting in yet another serious injury, he applied for a job at Manta Ray, a well-known restaurant at the beach. He spent six years there, first as a cook and then as a sous-chef, and knew that he had finally found his place – in the world of food.

In 2006, he cooked at a restaurant on the beach called Sea in Herzliya and in 2008 opened his own Libyan restaurant in the Neve Tzedek area. Initially it did quite well, but then the neighbourhood started changing and after four years the restaurant was no longer successful. And Benny had enough of cooking! His next experiment was producing snow cones, and for this he imported special ice-making machines from a company in Salt Lake City. He ran the business from home but soon saw that to be successful as an importer in Israel, you had to be big, which he wasn't. So he gave that up as well.

At that time, Benny lived near Levinsky Street and realised that the market didn't have a single good coffee place. That was the seed for his idea to open Café Levinsky 41, at the end of the market. He knew he didn't want a big place, so this kiosk was ideal. He designed the beautiful tiles, mirrors and glass of the interior himself. He has a financial partner named Moshe Priezement. The first year was tough, but Benny was sure it would work, and he turned out to be right: in recent years, more and more people have moved to this area. At home, he makes marzipan balls of various flavours to sell at his stand, but everything else he does on site.

While we down our delicious, healthy *gazoz*, Benny shares his plans for the future: he would like to write a book about drinks in Hebrew and English and is also thinking of expanding his business – to New York and Barcelona. We'll be paying attention.

COFFEE
1
COFFEE
LEV IN SKY

QUINCE JAM

RECIPE FROM BENNY BRIGA

For 3–4 jam jars

- 1 kg (2 lb 4 oz) quinces
- 500 g (1 lb 2 oz) sugar
- Several dried scented geranium leaves, or dried hibiscus blossoms

HAYA'S TIP:
THE JAM IS DELICIOUS ON FRESH BREAD, IN A CRUMBLE OR WITH PORRIDGE. IT ALSO GOES WELL WITH CHEESE AND ADDS A TOUCH OF SWEETNESS TO ASIAN RAGOUTS.

Thoroughly clean the quince and rub off the furry hairs. Then peel, deseed and cut into small cubes.

Place cubed quince in a saucepan, cover with sugar and leave for at least 2 days; the quince should take on a reddish-orange colour. Stir twice a day to evenly distribute the quince and sugar.

Place the saucepan on the stove and simmer the quince until the liquid has evaporated and the fruit is soft and dark red, about 2 hours. (If the quince are still too hard, add a bit of warm water and simmer a while longer.)

Ladle the hot jam into the sterilised screw-top jars, adding one scented geranium leaf to each. Seal the jars well, turn upside-down and allow to cool completely. Stored in the refrigerator, the jam will keep for at least 1 year.

ORANGE-OLIVE OIL CAKE

For a 28 cm (11 inch) cake

For the syrup:
- 500 ml (17 fl oz) freshly squeezed orange juice
- 350 g (12 oz) sugar
- 2 untreated oranges

For the batter:
- 4 eggs
- 250 g (9 oz) sugar
- 250 g (9 oz) Greek yoghurt
- 20 g (¾ oz) baking powder
- 220 ml (7½ fl oz) olive oil
- 220 ml (7½ fl oz) grape seed oil
- 450 g (1 lb) filo pastry

- 100 ml (3½ fl oz) cream, for whipping

For the *syrup*, bring the orange juice, sugar and 300 ml (10½ fl oz) water to the boil in a saucepan. Simmer over low heat for about 30 minutes, then remove from the heat. Pour off two-thirds of the liquid and set aside for pouring over the cake.

Peel one of the oranges with a vegetable peeler and cut the other into slices. Add the orange peel and slices to the liquid left in the pan. Simmer over heat until this has reduced to a thick syrup.

For the *batter*, preheat the oven to 200°C (400°F). Stir the eggs, sugar and yoghurt together in a bowl until combined and leave to rest for 10 minutes.

Stir in the baking powder, then slowly mix in both oils with a stick blender. Cut the filo pastry into 1 cm (½ inch) squares and gradually fold into the batter.

Line a 28 cm (11 inch) spring-form cake tin with baking paper, pour in the batter and bake for about 40 minutes.

Poke several holes in the top of the cake with a skewer. Pour the reserved orange juice mixture over the cake – it will seep into the holes and make the cake moist.

Whip the cream until it holds soft peaks. Glaze the cake with the syrup and serve with the whipped cream and the candied orange slices and peel from the syrup.

THE SOMMELIERS

Lewinsohn
GARAGE
DE
PAPA
Rouge 2014
Lewinsohn

NAAMA SZTERENLICHT, AVIRAM KATZ, JESSY BODEC

»The Sommeliers«

What could be better than spending a few relaxing hours with people who drink wine for a living? As we enter the small, cosy Halutzim 3 restaurant at the Levinsky Market, we are greeted by Naama. She is a sommelier here and partner in both life and in the restaurant with Eitan Vanunu, the chef of Halutzim 3.

The wine glasses are already waiting on our simple, but beautifully laid, little corner table. Aviram Katz and Jessy Bodec, two other sommeliers, join us, and today this trio will introduce us to the world of Israeli wines. Jessy, a friendly Frenchman who lived in Paris until he was 17, begins by explaining the origin of the word ›sommelier‹: it comes from *bête des sommes*, meaning ›beast of burden‹. Later this term was also used to refer to people who served beverages to the French king. It is not even noon but wine is served as if it were a matter of course. We begin with an Israeli white – delicious, crisp and dry.

It soon becomes clear that Aviram doesn't take himself too seriously. He describes with a grin how he drank vodka right from the bottle when he was 14 or 15. Only later did he become interested in what he was drinking and found wine, with its old world aura, to be his favourite. ›Unlike vodka,‹ he says, ›whose taste is unchanging, wine is always different.‹ The other sommeliers inform us – obviously proud of their friend and colleague – that in 2012, Aviram won the Yarden Prize, the most important national competition for sommeliers in Israel, but he is too modest to talk about it. In addition to his job as a sommelier, he works as the manager and host at HaBasta, a favourite spot for many epicures in Tel Aviv and a place where we, as well, felt very much at home (see page 160).

We empty our glasses and they are quickly refilled. Naama gained valuable experience in Italy working for the Slow Wine Guide and at various restaurants; she also attended the Slow Food University of Gastronomic Sciences in the Piedmont region. Naama learned a great deal about Israeli wines when she worked at Catit, a famous Tel Aviv restaurant. She speaks enthusiastically about the relationship between agriculture and nature: how you treat the land, the importance of the seasons, and the role of innovation and tradition. As she says: ›Wine is a means of transportation to take us to other times.‹ Although wine has long been cultivated here, Israel's wine industry is quite young. Nevertheless, interjects Jessy, ›the country has made immense progress in a relatively brief period of time.‹

Jessy took a different path to becoming a sommelier. His first experience with wine came while he was studying at Cornell University in New York. To help pay his college tuition, he applied for a job at a restaurant. The owner assumed that because of Jessy's French accent he would know something about wine. Jessy's interest was sparked and he took several wine classes at the university. Upon returning to Israel, he worked in various restaurants, including the famous Keren, before venturing out on his own.

»To be a sommelier, you must be a gourmet; you must love good food.«

We want to know more about Israeli wines, such as how they became fashionable in this country. Aviram provides us with a brief history of modern winemaking. Rothschild's Carmel Winery, established at the end of the 19th century, was a pioneer in this regard: ›Over a hundred years later,‹ he remarks, ›we now have good wine.‹ Dr. Cornelius Ough, a renowned professor from the University of California (U.C. Davis), visited Israel in 1972 and found the land and the climate in the area surrounding the Golan Heights to be superbly suited for vineyards. Now wine-growing areas are to be found even in Israel's desert. The so-called first wine revolution, in 1983, is considered the beginning of modern Israeli wines. At the beginning of this millennium, the second Israeli wine revolution started taking shape. ›Everybody started producing high-quality wines,‹ explains Aviram. ›This was again a time of great progress.‹ Aviram also calls this development the ›quality revolution‹.

Eitan, Naama's good-humoured husband, brings various dishes to our table that perfectly match the wine. We enjoy a lentil salad with chickweed, coriander (cilantro), goat's milk yoghurt and chilli. This is followed by warm, fragrant bread and a plate filled with three kinds of beans, feta-like Israeli goat's cheese and pumpkin strips marinated in verjuice. Naama and Eitan explain that verjuice is made from the unripe red grapes that cannot be used for winemaking.

We continue to leisurely eat, drink and chat. Jessy, who in 2005 won the Yarden Sommelier Prize as well, talks about the wanderlust of many Israelis, which is due in large part to the existential and political problems in the country. Many return with a greater appreciation for wine and good food and begin to invest. Despite all the progress, wine consumption per capita in Israel is not that high: only about seven litres per capita annually. We learn that there is still a widespread assumption here that wine should be drunk only on special occasions – which Aviram takes great pleasure in contradicting: ›You should really be drinking wine on Monday evening to go with your simple scrambled eggs.‹ We find Aviram's attitude a refreshing change from the snobbery often found in Europe's professional wine circles: ›At least 95% of wines in the world are drinkable, so you should just enjoy them!‹ he says. Jessy tells us that the average Israeli drinks mostly semi-dry red wine, which is why education and a good selection of other wine varieties are so

important – and not only in high-end restaurants. We return to the subject of the significance of wine. Jessy talks about how winegrowing helps connect the earth with people, and that people are changed in this process. And with no other drink, he continues, do you have this close link between the climate and the soil. Aviram also talks about connections and the search for identity: ›Wine is shaped by place, as it is always local; by time, because the vintage is different each year; and by the people who produce it.‹

Our glasses are empty. We finish by asking our three sommeliers about their favourite wineries in Israel. Here are their tips:

Aviram: Château Golan, Lewinsohn, Mia Luce
Jessy: Agur, Bar-Maor, Bialik (his own wine), Domaine du Castel, Clos de Gat, Pelter, Ramat Negev, Shvo, Tzora, Vortman
Naama: Abaya, Château Golan, Lewinsohn, Shvo, Tzora

RECIPE INDEX

GLOSSARY

AMBA
A sweet-sour mango pickle condiment from Indian grocers.

BAHARAT
An Arabic spice blend usually made with pepper, paprika, cinnamon and pimento. ›Baharat‹ is the Arabic word for ›spices‹.

BRANZINO
European sea bass.

BULGUR
Parboiled and ground durum wheat. It can be served like rice as a side dish and is also a good filling for vegetables.

BUREKA VS BURIKA
The difference between bureka and burika, aside from the one letter in their spelling, lies in the kind of dough used and the preparation: burekas are usually made with puff pastry and baked in the oven, while burikas are prepared with paper-thin sheets of dough that are stuffed and deep-fried until crisp.

BUTTER BEANS
Large white beans that probably originated in Peru, also known as lima beans. White jack beans are a suitable substitute.

CHALLA
A braided bread commonly eaten on Shabbat or Jewish holidays.

CHIMICHURRI
A South American sauce made from herbs, spices, vinegar and oil.

DATE SYRUP
Date syrup is often available at Middle Eastern groceries or organic supermarkets. You can also make it yourself: simply purée dried dates with a bit of water until you have a thick paste.

FREEKEH
Durum wheat grains harvested while still green and then roasted. A suitable substitute is ›Grünkern‹, unripe spelt grains.

GALANGAL
A rhizome, similar to ginger, with a flavour that is both fresh and spicy. Galangal is available fresh and as a powder. It is an important component in Thai spice pastes.

HARISSA
A spicy North African paste made of chillies and various seasonings.

IKRA
Carp roe.

KAFFIR LIME
A small citrus fruit yielding little juice. The fruit itself does not play an important role in cooking, but the very aromatic leaves of the plant are frequently used. The name is controversial, as ›Kaffir‹ is also a derogatory term for black people in countries including South Africa. The fruit is called ›makrut lime‹ as well, which is less offensive but less well known.

KATAIFI
Thin strings of pastry, also known as angel hair, usually made with a sweet filling. Often available at Middle Eastern supermarkets.

LAHOH
A Yemeni bread that, like tortillas, is fried in a pan.

MEDJOOL DATES
An especially sweet variety of date originally from Morocco, now also grown in Israel, Palestine, Iraq, California and South Africa.

MERGUEZ
Spicy sausage from North Africa. Good substitutes are chorizo and salsiccia (spicy Italian sausage).

MIRIN
A sweet Japanese rice wine.

MISO PASTE
A paste consisting of fermented soya beans and a number of other ingredients as seasonings. The miso made with red fermented rice has a pungent flavour, while the white miso has more of a sweet and subtle taste.

MUSCOVADO SUGAR
Dark, slightly sticky raw cane sugar. Brown sugar is a substitute.

OKRA
A plant bearing edible seed pods whose taste is similar to green beans. When prepared, the pods should not be sliced so deeply that the inside chambers are visible, or they can collapse when cooked and become slimy.

PALM SUGAR
A sugar with a malty taste derived from the boiled-down sap of various palm trees.

PANEER
An Indian fresh cheese that retains its shape when heated. Usually available at Indian supermarkets.

SEA SALT
We use a medium grain sea salt; kosher salt is a good alternative.

SENIA
A large, flat pan with two handles. Can occasionally be found at Turkish shops selling housewares. Use any very large pan or a large round cake tin.

SIVRI
A green, hot Turkish pepper that, along with olive oil, is the secret star of this book.

SUMAC
The fruits of the sumac plant are also known as ›lemonade berries‹, and they have a very sour flavour. In Middle Eastern cookery the ground berries are mixed with a bit of salt and sprinkled on salads in place of vinegar or lemon.

TAHINI
A thick paste made of sesame seeds, available at Middle Eastern groceries. As well as the product made especially for us in Palestine, we like Lebanese tahini.

TAMARIND PASTE
A sour fruity paste made from the pulp of the tamarind fruit. Aailable at international supermarkets.

ZA'ATAR
A very spicy herb with flavour similar to oregano, thyme and marjoram. Fresh oregano is a suitable substitute. Za'atar also refers to a spice mixture made from that herb, sesame, sumac and salt. Nearly every region has its own recipe: sometimes cumin is added, sometimes a bit of thyme. The za'atar mixture goes well with salads and cheese and is often served with a bit of olive oil and bread for dipping.

ZHUG
A Yemeni spice mixture made of herbs, chillies and garlic.

THE TEAM

HAYA

Haya Molcho loves cooking and travelling. Born in Tel Aviv, she has lived in many different places. She was constantly on the move during much of her life, first as a child with her parents, then as an adult on her own, and later with her husband, the mime artist Samy Molcho. Cooking is Haya's great passion. During her travels she got to know the cuisines of the world and developed her own unique culinary style, which is typically Israeli and at the same time international. In March 2009 she and her sons opened their restaurant NENI at Vienna's Naschmarkt – a success story from the very beginning. For *Tel Aviv: Food – People – Stories*, she and the NENI team prepared beloved dishes from her native country and allowed the residents of Tel Aviv to have their say as well in order to capture the city's very special atmosphere and attitude towards life.

NURIEL

Nuriel Molcho is Haya's oldest son, co-founder of NENI. He is responsible for marketing and PR as well as for designing concepts for additional locations. Like his father, Samy, he is a born aesthete: he loves architecture, art and fashion and lives out this passion through photography. He travels a great deal for his work and describes himself as a *nomade moderne*, which is also the name of his own hat label.

ELIHAY

Elihay Biran was born in France and grew up with his mother and brother in the Israeli desert. They travelled a great deal, leading a kind of modern nomadic life that continues to influence him. He got his first taste of kitchen work at an early age at one of Israel's best restaurants and discovered cooking as his means of expressing himself. He worked in cities including Tel Aviv and Paris, where he met Haya, Nuriel and Ilan Molcho. For three years he was head of the international kitchen team at NENI, and in this period the Molchos became his second family. He currently has plans for opening his own restaurant in Vienna, in partnership with NENI.

ELLEN

Ellen Lewis taught literature for over 35 years at international schools in Austria, Italy and Belgium and after her retirement from teaching lived for a time in Egypt. As a transplanted Californian, she has made Europe her home for the past 40 years and now enjoys life in Provence. She still spends time working with young people as an educational consultant and has been involved in numerous writing projects. Her close friendship with Haya began 20 years ago in Vienna, when Haya oversaw the culinary side of the bat mitzvahs of Ellen and Walther's daughters. The Molchos have now become part of the family.

THE TEAM

WALTHER

After many years as a teacher and director at international schools in New York, Vienna, Duino (Italy), Brussels, Abu Dhabi and Cairo, Walther Hetzer now enjoys a very active ›retirement‹ in Provence (France), discovering regional wines, tapenade and countless varieties of goat's and sheep's cheese. As director of the Vienna International School, he got to know all four of the Molcho sons when they were pupils there. Since then, he and his wife Ellen have been close friends of the family. Their collaboration on this book led not only to a few newly gained pounds but also to new friends on the NENI team.

LAURA

Laura Karasinski, Vienna-born with roots in Poland, is an art director, designer and head of Atelier Karasinski, which she founded in 2012. Art, design and travel are passions she shares with the Molcho family, with whom she loves to explore the world for both business and pleasure, discovering new cultures, tastes and stories along the way.

MARIE

Marie-Therese Burka was born and raised in Vienna. In 2012 she became part of the NENI team: she started off working at Tel Aviv Beach and since 2015 has been responsible for marketing and event management. She loves travelling, exploring new cultures and foods from all over the world, and taking pictures in order to capture magical moments. For her, NENI is more than just a job; it is also a place where she works with people who are almost family to her. Discovering little-known places on the joint trip to Tel Aviv only served to intensify her love for this extraordinary city.

DOUGLAS

Born in Ohio, USA, Douglas Deitemyer came to Vienna as a music student and has since lived and worked here as a musician, music teacher and freelance translator, with an emphasis on history, culture and food.

ADRIAN

Adrian Hadary was born and raised in Israel. His great love brought him to Vienna seven years ago, which is also when he began working with Haya. Six years ago he became executive chef of NENI on Naschmarkt, and since 2017 he has been a member of the franchise team, overseeing all NENI restaurants. He discovered his love of cooking as a child in his grandmother's kitchen and since then has lived this passion every day.

Published in 2019 by Murdoch Books, an imprint of Allen & Unwin
First published in 2018 by Christian Brandstätter Verlag, Vienna

Murdoch Books Australia
83 Alexander Street, Crows Nest NSW 2065
Phone: +61 (0)2 8425 0100
murdochbooks.com.au
info@murdochbooks.com.au

Murdoch Books UK
Ormond House, 26–27 Boswell Street, London WC1N 3JZ
Phone: +44 (0) 20 8785 5995
murdochbooks.co.uk
info@murdochbooks.co.uk

For corporate orders and custom publishing contact
our business development team at salesenquiries@murdochbooks.com.au

Publisher: Corinne Roberts
English language editors: Justin Wolfers & Jane Price
Recipes: Haya Molcho & Elihay Biran
Story text: Ellen Lewis & Walther Hetzer
Photography: Nuriel Molcho
Editorial staff: Marie Burka, Jonathan Bergman, Adrian Hadary
Translator: Douglas Deitemyer
Art Direction & Design: Atelier Karasinski
Layout: Luisa Franz Kleopatra Klobassa
Production Director: Lou Playfair

ISBN 978 1 76052 390 9 Australia
ISBN 978 1 76063 467 4 UK

A cataloguing-in-publication entry is available from the
catalogue of the National Library of Australia at nla.gov.au
A catalogue record for this book is available from the British Library

Colour reproduction by Splitting Image Colour Studio Pty Ltd, Clayton, Victoria
Printed by C & C Offset Printing, China

The paper in this book is FSC® certified.
FSC® promotes environmentally responsible,
socially beneficial and economically viable
management of the world's forests.

www.neni.at

2015